TOP 200 Dessert Recipes (

Written by: Jamie Stewart

Copyright © 2015

All Rights Reserved

Warning-Disclaimer

Table Of Contents

Introduction

It is hard to imagine a great family lunch without any dessert! Holidays, family gathering, New Year's Eve, birthday party and so on – these are events that remind us of the good cake, cookies or other brilliant desserts. When we imagine a festive table, we immediately think of a dish that will indulge our sweet tooth. If you are able to read grandma's secret notebook, you will certainly find a lot of recipes for authentic desserts that are passed down through the generations. Indeed, dessert is "must-make" if you want to cheer up your family and friends!

Simple Ideas for Amazing Desserts

"200 Dessert Recipes Cookbook" is designed to satisfy both skilled bakers and very beginners. There are fundamental dessert recipes and zippy recipes that every home cook should know, as well as innovative, insanely good recipes that you've always wanted to know. Give your lunch the perfect ending with one of these admirable recipes!

What's the catch? This cookbook is inspired by traditional values and specific mission: get back to home cooking and baking! Of course, you can always buy the cake or go to the candy shop. However, when you prepare the cake for your child's birthday or anniversary, it is a special feeling, irreplaceable, wonderful! The most expensive and the best store-bought cake you can purchase does not have a very important ingredient – your love!

The other important vision of this book is: learn to bake and prepare the sweets on an easy and fun way. Every recipe includes detailed step-by-step instructions for preparation. Moreover, culinary terms are clear and precise, so that even beginners can find their way. In any case, it is good to mention some useful hints to get started.

Keep some pieces of baking equipment handy. These are:

Baking non-stick (parchment) paper which is moisture-proof and greaseproof.

Cooling rack

Food mixer and Food processor

Mixing bowls

Pastry brush

Rolling pin

Scales

Spatula, Whisk and Spoons

There are ingredients every home baker should always have in his/her baker's pantry:

All-purpose flour, cornstarch or gluten-free flour (if needed)

Sugars (white, brown and powdered sugar) and Honey

Baking soda and Baking powder

Seasonal fruit, Citrus fruit and Dried fruits

Nut butter

Shortening, neutral cooking oil and butter (or margarine)

Eggs

Nuts

If you glimpse the recipes in this cookbook, you can see that they are full of fantastic and aromatic spices. Here is a little guide to spices and herbs that will teach you to make desserts like a professional chef:

Cinnamon can be used in almost every baking recipe, sweet and savory. Actually, this is an extremely healthy spice that was found to have a positive effect on blood sugar control, cancer prevention, osteoporosis prevention, and so on.

Cardamom is commonly used cooking spice and flavoring in desserts; therefore, you can find it in these recipes.

Vanilla extract goes well with fruits, puddings, whipped topping, and ice creams.

Anise seed can be used in spiced cookies, waffles, compotes, jellies. and similar desserts.

Allspice is widely used in both savory recipes and dessert recipes. Allspice matches well with sweet bread, stuffed apples, cheese frosting, spiced cider, pumpkin cheesecake, ginger cookies, and so on.

Cloves reminds on winter, Oriental treats, and mulled wine. It goes well in spiced tea, spiced compote, molasses cookies, gingerbread, baked banana, pumpkin shortbread, baklava, honey cake, etc. Its scent is simply saying irresistible!

Mace gives great pleasant flavor to your desserts. Mace can be used in bakery foods like cookies, cakes, pastries as well as fruit crisps, spiced tea, donuts, gingerbread, fruit pie, and so on.

Ginger matches well with yogurt desserts, various of cookies, dessert pies, cakes, and so on.

Nutmeg is commonly used flavoring in many recipes, both savory and sweet. Put freshly ground nutmeg into your smoothies, cookies, cakes, muffins, baked apples or bananas, or aromatic coffee and you will be delighted by specific aromas and gorgeous flavors.

Chinese Five-spice powder goes well with fruits and crèmes. You can use it to prepare fantastic, memorable chocolate recipes, apple pies, Thanksgiving recipes, etc.

At the very beginning, stick to the recommendations and the ingredients that are listed in any of the recipes. Later, as you progress, you can create a unique, fanciful desserts by adding your own combination of spices. Therefore, spice it up and you will see a big difference!

Delicious Recipes to Satisfy Your Sweet Tooth

You've decided to learn how to make the best desserts. If you are an absolute beginner, it is best to simplify things. Therefore, try to start from easy recipes such as three-ingredient or four-ingredient desserts, simple puddings, quick fruit salads, and super-fast microwave cakes. Of course, you will find a lot of easy desserts in the cookbook. Read and follow recipes thoughtfully and you will succeed.

Cakes tend to be more effort and take more experience and skills. Pastries are even more difficult to prepare than cookies and cakes. Of course, it is best to go step by step before you feel confident to make fancier cakes such as croissants, birthday cakes or layered cakes.

Among other things, you must know your oven. In the beginning, it is best to bake cakes in the center of the oven (middle rack). In terms of oven temperature, follow the instructions that are provided in the recipe. In the majority of recipes, you should preheat your oven about 15 minutes before baking.

Purchase a good kitchen scale in order to measure ingredients accurately.

Make sure to use a suitable and properly sized baking dishes, cookie pans, and pie plates.

Unless otherwise listed, when baking cake, rotate it after 20 minutes.

On the other hand, if you are a skilled baker, you can try new twists on classic cakes and cookies! As you can see, we took grandmother's recipes that are prepared in the traditional way and adapted them to a modern chef. Some of the recipes take a little time, 10 or 15 minutes; some of the recipes take a few hours. It gives you the ability to plan your time. Every recipe includes preparation time and the number of servings.

Healthy Dessert Ideas – Give it a Try!

If you want to lose weight, if you are allergic to some ingredients, or if you just take care of diet, you don't have to give up your dessert. The cookbook contains fifty healthy and diet-friendly recipes you can make anywhere. Check out our easy recipes that can help you to cut down on sugar and the other unhealthy ingredients. You will find a lot of healthier ways to satisfy your sweet tooth by making these amazing desserts. You can substitute honey for sugar, peanut butter for chocolate cream, fresh fruits for candied fruits, dark chocolate for milk chocolate, and so on.

There are a lot of healthy dessert choices, much more than you can imagine. Yogurt Parfait, Smoothie, Cinnamon Toast, Frozen Fruits with Yogurt, Fruit Popsicles, Sorbet, Baked Apple, Low-Fat Pudding, Flavored Greek Yogurt, and so on. The possibilities are unlimited! We recommend these fifty recipes just enough to inspire you and remind you that life is too short to eat bad desserts.

Contrary to the general belief, the desserts are unexpectedly good for our health and we should not skip them every time. Of course, you should not eat dessert every day, but you should pamper yourself from time to time. Listen to your body, it is good for your mental health. High carbohydrate food helps our brain and body to produce various hormones and substances that cause the feeling of happiness. Many studies have shown that people who eat healthy food and who eat rich desserts have better success in weight loss. It's because the body feels satisfied. If you don't eat dessert, you will limit your intake of carbohydrates which can cause the deficit of glucose. And glucose provides energy for our body Finally, desserts include carbohydrates. And carbohydrates are one of the essential nutrients. It is important to make good choices and stay away from empty calories.

When you serve a great dessert to someone and he/she is thrilled, that person may ask you: "What is your secret?" Just smile and say: "Love is my secret ingredient! I made it with all my heart". Indeed, this is true. Everything that is truly good comes from love. This cookbook is created to inspire you and teach you to cook with love!

Chocolate Peppermint Bars

(Ready in about 2 hours 25 minutes | Servings 20)

Ingredients

For the Bottom Layer:

Non-stick cooking spray

1 cup pastry flour

1 cup sugar

A pinch of salt

1/2 cup egg substitute

1/4 cup margarine, melted

2 tablespoons water

1/4 teaspoon allspice

2 large-sized eggs, beaten

1 (16-ounce) can chocolate syrup

For the Peppermint Layer:

2 cups powdered sugar

2 tablespoons whole milk

1/4 cup margarine, melted

3/4 teaspoon pure peppermint extract

For the Chocolate Glaze:

3/4 cup chocolate chips of choice

3 tablespoons margarine

Directions

Begin by preheating an oven to 350 degrees F. Spray a baking pan with non-stick cooking spray in order to grease slightly.

To make the bottom layer, add the flour to a measuring cup; level with a knife. Add the sugar, salt and egg substitute; whisk to combine.

In another mixing bowl, combine together 1/4 cup margarine, 2 tablespoons water, allspice, eggs, and chocolate syrup; mix until smooth. Add the flour mixture to this wet mixture. Stir until the mixture is well blended.

Pour the batter into greased baking. Bake until a wooden pick inserted in center comes out almost clean or approximately 25 minutes. Allow to cool completely.

To make the peppermint layer, combine powdered sugar, whole milk, margarine, and peppermint extract. Beat with an electric mixer until the mixture is creamy and smooth. Next, spread peppermint mixture over prepared cake.

To make the glaze: Melt chocolate chips and 3 tablespoons of margarine in a microwave oven. Allow to stand for 2 minutes.

Then, spread the chocolate glaze evenly over top of your cake. Cut into squares, serve, and enjoy!

Quick and Easy Cherry Crisp

(Ready in about 20 minutes | Servings 4)

Ingredients

1/3 cup granulated sugar

1 tablespoon corn flour

4 cups cherries, pitted

1 teaspoon almond extract

1 cup cookies, crumbled

2 tablespoons butter, softened

1/4 cup almonds, toasted and coarsely chopped

Directions

In a mixing bowl, combine together granulated sugar and corn flour. Transfer to a large-sized sauté pan; add the cherries and stir to combine.

Cook over medium heat, 10 to 12 minutes, until the mixture is thickened and bubbly.

In a medium-sized mixing bowl, thoroughly combine the rest of the ingredients.

Divide cherry mixture among 4 dessert bowls. Sprinkle with cookie mixture and enjoy!

Apple and Pear Crisp with Ice Cream

(Ready in about 1 hour | Servings 6)

Ingredients

6 medium-sized apples, peeled, cored and cut into chunks

4 medium-sized pears, peeled, cored and cut into chunks

1 teaspoon lemon zest, grated

1/2 cup brown sugar

1/4 cup all-purpose flour

1/2 teaspoon dry ginger, grated

1/2 teaspoon ground nutmeg

1 teaspoon ground cinnamon

3 tablespoons orange juice, freshly squeezed

Vanilla ice cream, as garnish

Directions

Begin by preheating your oven to 350 degrees F.

Put the apples and pears into a large-sized mixing bowl. Then, sprinkle with lemon zest, brown sugar, flour, ginger, nutmeg, and cinnamon. Drizzle with orange juice.

Pour into a baking dish. Bake about 50 minutes, or until the top of crisp is bubbly.

Divide among eight dessert dishes. Serve warm with a dollop of vanilla ice cream.

Walnut and Marshmallow Parfaits

(Ready in about 20 minutes | Servings 4)

Ingredients

1 chocolate fudge instant pudding mix

2 cups whole milk

1/2 teaspoon ground cinnamon

1/2 teaspoon anise seed

1/2 cup whipped dessert topping

1/4 cup walnuts, chopped

1/4 cup miniature marshmallows

Chocolate shavings, as garnish

Directions

First of all, prepare the pudding mix with milk, cinnamon and anise seed according to package directions.

Transfer 3/4 cup of the prepared pudding to a mixing bowl; fold in whipped dessert topping. Mix until the mixture is well combined.

Put the remaining chocolate pudding into the nice dessert dishes. Then, top with dessert topping mixture.

Sprinkle with walnuts and miniature marshmallows. Top with chocolate shavings. Eat chilled!

Walnut Raisin Cake

(Ready in about 40 minutes | Servings 8)

Ingredients

1 yellow cake mix

1/2 teaspoon pure vanilla extract

1 teaspoon coconut extract

1 cup walnuts, coarsely chopped

1 cup golden raisins

1 1/3 cup evaporated milk

1 1/3 cup white sugar

1/2 cup butter, softened

4 egg yolks, slightly beaten

1 package whipped cream, as garnish

Toasted shaved coconut, as garnish

Directions

Begin by baking the yellow cake as directed. Bake with vanilla and coconut extract.

To make the filling: combine walnuts, raisins, milk, sugar, butter, egg yolks in a medium-sized saucepan. Allow to cook over medium heat until your filling is thickened.

Next, split the cake layers; spread prepared walnut filling on each layer.

Frost your cake with whipped cream and sprinkle with shaved coconut. Serve chilled and enjoy!

Delicious Almond and Figs Cake

(Ready in about 40 minutes | Servings 8)

Ingredients

1 package white cake mix	1 1/3 cup sugar
1 teaspoon pure hazelnut extract	1 1/3 cup evaporated milk
1 teaspoon pure vanilla extract	1/2 cup butter, softened
1 cup almonds, coarsely chopped	4 egg yolks, beaten
1 cup figs, chopped	1 package whipped cream, as garnish

Directions

Bake white cake mix in a preheated oven, adding hazelnut extract and vanilla extract. Bake according to manufacturer's instructions.

To prepare the filling: in a saucepan, mix together the almonds, figs, sugar and milk; stir until everything is well blended.

Then, stir in softened butter and egg yolks. Cook over medium heat about 15 minutes or until the filling is thickened.

Then, split prepared cake layers; spread your filling on each layer.

Frost the entire cake with whipped cream. Set in a fridge before cutting and serving. Divide among dessert plates and enjoy.

Fluffy Raisin Almond Bars

(Ready in about 50 minutes | Servings 12)

Ingredients

2 sticks butter

1/2 cup white sugar

1 teaspoon molasses

3/4 cup brown sugar

2 cups all-purpose flour

2 cups rolled oats

1/2 teaspoon baking powder

1/2 teaspoon baking soda

A pinch of salt

1 teaspoon pure coconut extract

1/2 cup almonds, chopped and toasted

1 cup golden raisins

2/3 cup corn syrup

3/4 cup water

Coconut shavings, as garnish

Directions

Begin by preheating an oven to 350 degrees F. Grease a baking dish with non-stick cooking spray or with melted butter.

In a mixing bowl, beat together butter, white sugar, molasses, brown sugar until the mixture is uniform and fluffy.

In another mixing bowl, stir together flour, rolled oats, baking powder, baking soda, salt, coconut extract, and almonds.

Add this mixture to the beaten butter mixture; stir to combine. Reserve 1 ½ cup of the mixture for topping. Press remaining mixture into the bottom of greased baking dish; bake for 15 minutes.

Meanwhile, combine golden raisins, corn syrup and water in a medium-sized saucepan. Cook over medium heat, bringing to a boil.

Decrease the heat to medium-low and continue cooking 10 minutes longer. Spread raisin mixture over the baked layer. Spread reserved mixture over the top of the cake.

Bake for another 15 minutes. Allow to cool completely before cutting and serving. Garnish with prepared coconut shavings. Enjoy!

Pumpkin Pie with Candied Walnuts

(Ready in about 1 hour | Servings 12)

Ingredients

For the Crust:

2 cups crushed ginger snap cookies

1 tablespoon dark molasses

1/4 cup granulated sugar

1 stick butter, melted

For the Pie Filling:

1 (15-ounce) canned pumpkin purée

1 (12-ounce) can of evaporated milk

3/4 cup granulated sugar

3 medium-sized eggs, lightly beaten

1 teaspoon anise seed

1 teaspoon pumpkin pie spice

For the Topping:

1/2 stick butter, softened

1/2 cup walnuts, toasted and coarsely chopped

1/4 cup sugar

Directions

In a mixing bowl, combine all the above ingredients for the Crust. Then, press the mixture into a pie plate.

Next, preheat an oven to 350 degrees F.

Next, make the Pie Filling. Mix together canned pumpkin purée, evaporated milk, 3/4 cup granulated sugar, eggs, anise seed and pumpkin pie spice; mix until smooth and creamy. Pour the pie filling into pie crust.

In a sauté pan, melt the butter over medium heat. Add walnuts and sugar. Cook over low heat for 5 minutes.

Bake in the preheated oven until the center of the pie is set or about 50 minutes. Let cool slightly before cutting and serving.

Nutty Chocolate Bars

(Ready in about 30 minutes | Servings 12)

Ingredients

1/2 cup butter

2 cups nut butter

1 package crushed graham crackers

1/4 teaspoon grated nutmeg

1/4 teaspoon ground cinnamon

3 cups confectioners' sugar

2 cups semisweet chocolate chips

1/2 cup butter

Directions

In a saucepan, melt together 1/2 cup butter and 2 cups nut butter over medium heat.

Turn off the heat. Add crushed graham crackers, nutmeg, cinnamon, and confectioners' sugar. Press this nutty mixture into a shallow square plate.

To make the topping, melt together 2 cups semisweet chocolate chips and 1/2 cup butter.

Pour the chocolate topping over warm nutty base. Allow to cool completely; then, cut into bars. Enjoy!

Amazing Kids-Friendly Snowballs

(Ready in about 45 minutes | Servings 10)

Ingredients

2 sticks butter, softened

1/2 cup powdered sugar

1/2 teaspoon pure almond extract

1/2 teaspoon pure coconut extract

2 ½ cups all-purpose flour

2 tablespoons cream cheese, softened

1 tablespoon water

1/2 cup white sugar

8 tablespoons finely crushed candy canes

1-2 drops food coloring of choice

1/4 cup powdered sugar

Directions

In a medium-sized mixing bowl, beat together the butter and 1/2 cup of powdered sugar; add almond extract and coconut extract.

Next, stir in the flour; knead by hands until the mixture is well combined. Set aside 1/2 cup of the dough. Shape remaining dough into bite-sized balls. Create a well in the center of each ball.

To make the filling, mix together the cream cheese and 1 tablespoon of water. Add 1/2 cup of white sugar, 2 tablespoons crushed candy canes and food coloring of choice; mix until everything is well blended.

Fill the balls with creamy filling. Then, use reserved dough to cover the filling.

Bake in preheated oven at 350 degrees F for about 14 minutes.

In a shallow bowl, place remaining 6 tablespoons of crushed candy canes and 1/4 cup of powdered sugar; roll warm cookies in this mixture. Then, place the cookies on a wire rack in order to cool completely.

Transfer the cookies to a nice serving platter and serve!

Easy Raspberry Date Bars

(Ready in about 45 minutes | Servings 12)

Ingredients

1 ½ cups raspberries, fresh or frozen

1 cup dates, chopped

2 tablespoons water

2 cups flour

2 cups old-fashioned oats

1 ½ cups packed brown sugar

1/2 teaspoon baking powder

A pinch of salt

1/4 teaspoon ground cinnamon

1/4 teaspoon grated nutmeg

1/4 teaspoon ground cloves

2 sticks butter, melted

For the Glaze:

2 cups confectioners' sugar

3 tablespoons orange juice

1/2 teaspoon vanilla extract

Directions

In a skillet, simmer raspberries, dates and water over low heat for 15 minutes, stirring occasionally. Set aside.

In a large-sized mixing bowl, combine together the flour, oats, brown sugar, baking powder and a pinch of salt. Stir in the cinnamon, nutmeg, cloves, and melted butter; stir until everything is well blended.

Pat half of the mixture into a baking pan. Bake at 350 degrees F for about 10 minutes.

Spoon raspberry mixture over crust. Sprinkle with remaining flour mixture. Bake an additional 30 minutes. Allow to cool completely. Cut into bars.

In a small-sized bowl, combine glaze ingredients; drizzle the glaze over cooled bars and serve.

Best Sweet Empanadas Ever

(Ready in about 35 minutes | Servings 12)

Ingredients

8 ¾ cups all-purpose flour

2 pounds lard

8 teaspoons sugar

2 teaspoons salt

2 cups cold water

Jam of choice, as filling

Directions

Place flour and lard in a large-sized mixing bowl; add the sugar and salt. Mix with your fingers.

Add water and stir again until everything is well combined. Then, make the empanadas and flatten them. Fill them with your favorite jam.

Next, crimp the edges of your empanadas. Transfer to the baking pan; bake in a preheated oven at 300 degrees F, for about 30 minutes. Serve and enjoy!

Old-Fashioned Almond Cookies

(Ready in about 25 minutes | Servings 12)

Ingredients

2 sticks butter

1/2 cup powdered sugar

2 cups all-purpose flour

A pinch of salt

1 cup slivered almonds, toasted

1/2 teaspoon ground cinnamon

1 teaspoon pure vanilla extract

Icing sugar, for garnish

Directions

Start by preheating an oven to 350 degrees F.

In a mixing bowl, combine together the butter and sugar. Add flour and salt; stir to combine.

Then, add the toasted almonds, cinnamon, and pure vanilla extract. Mix to combine and knead by hands.

Shape the dough into the balls and transfer them to a baking tray. Bake about 15 minutes in the preheated oven. Dust with icing sugar and serve.

Country Soft Apple Pie

(Ready in about 55 minutes | Servings 8)

Ingredients

3/4 cup granulated sugar	1 cup flour
1/4 cup self-rising flour	1/2 cup butter
1/2 teaspoon anise seed	1/4 teaspoon pure vanilla extract
1/2 teaspoon cinnamon	1/2 cup packed brown sugar

6 apples, peeled, cored and sliced

Directions

To make the pie crust shell: In a mixing bowl, combine together 3/4 cup granulated sugar, 1/4 cup flour, anise seed, cinnamon, and apples.

Mix by fingers until everything is well incorporated. Transfer to a baking dish.

To make the topping: In another mixing bowl, combine the flour, butter, vanilla extract, and brown sugar.

Bake in the preheated oven at 400 degrees F, approximately 45 minutes, or until the pie is golden brown. Allow to cool slightly before cutting into slices. Enjoy!

Mom's Puffy Sugar Cookies

(Ready in about 20 minutes + chilling time | Servings 16)

Ingredients

4 cups all-purpose flour	2 sticks butter
1/2 teaspoon baking soda	1 ½ cup sugar
1 teaspoon baking powder	1 large-sized egg
A pinch of salt	1/2 cup sour cream
1/2 teaspoon ground cinnamon	1 teaspoon orange rind
1/2 teaspoon grated nutmeg	1 teaspoon pure vanilla extract

Directions

Start by preheating an oven to 375 degrees F. Line a cookie sheet with a baking paper or silicone baking mat.

Sift together flour, baking soda, baking powder, and salt. Add ground cinnamon and grated nutmeg.

Using an electric mixer, cream the butter, sugar and egg at medium speed. Mix till the mixture is light and fluffy. Turn the speed to low; add sour cream, orange rind, and pure vanilla extract. Mix until smooth.

Gradually and slowly add dry mixture, beating until everything is well blended. Shape the mixture into a ball. Then, set in a refrigerator 8 to 9 hours or overnight.

Roll the dough out on floured board. Then, cut out with a cookie cutter.

Bake about 12 minutes. Transfer to a cooling rack before serving time.

Mother's Day Chocolate Truffles

(Ready in about 20 minutes + chilling time | Servings 12)

Ingredients

1 ½ cups chocolate

3/4 cup heavy whipping cream

2 tablespoons butter, softened

1/4 cup chili powder

1/4 cup Kahlua

1/2 cup cocoa powder

Directions

Put the chocolate into a steel bowl.

In a medium-sized saucepan, heat heavy whipping cream, butter, and chili powder over medium flame; then, bring to a boil. Pour over chocolate in the steel bowl.

Pour Kahlua into the bowl. Allow to rest about 5 minutes. Whisk gently to combine. Set aside in a refrigerator for about 8 hours or overnight.

Place the cocoa powder onto a shallow plate. Then, scoop out the chocolate and form small-sized balls. Roll the balls in the cocoa powder. Line a cookie sheet with a sheet of wax paper.

Transfer to your freezer. You can sprinkle chili powder over chilled truffles if desired.

Easiest Yummiest Fluffy Cake

(Ready in about 1 hour | Servings 12)

Ingredients

4 large-sized eggs, lightly beaten

1 teaspoon lemon zest

1/4 teaspoon grated nutmeg

1/4 teaspoon ground cinnamon

1/4 teaspoon ground mace

1 cup sour cream

1/2 cup water

1/2 cup canola oil

1 chocolate cake mix

1 small box instant chocolate pudding

1 ½ cups chocolate chips

Directions

Begin by preheating an oven to 350 degrees F.

Combine together the eggs, lemon zest, nutmeg, cinnamon, mace, sour cream, water, and canola oil in a mixing bowl.

Add chocolate cake mix, instant chocolate pudding, and chocolate chips.

Bake approximately 1 hour. You can sift powdered sugar on top if desired. Indulge your sweet tooth!

Halloween Pumpkin and Pecan Treat

(Ready in about 1 hour | Servings 18)

Ingredients

Non-stick cooking spray

1 package yellow cake mix

1/3 cup margarine, at room temperature

4 eggs, lightly beaten

1 (29-ounce) can pumpkin

1/2 cup sugar

2/3 cup milk

1/2 teaspoon ground mace

1 tablespoon pumpkin pie spice

1/4 cup margarine, chilled

1/2 cup sugar

3/4 cup pecans, chopped

Ice cream, as garnish

Directions

Begin by preheating an oven to 350 degrees F. Then, lightly grease a 9x13 inch baking dish with non-stick cooking spray.

Reserve 1 cup of yellow cake mix. In a mixing bowl, combine remaining yellow cake mix with 1/3 cup of margarine and 1 egg; mix until everything is well combined.

Spread the cake mix mixture in the bottom of the greased baking dish.

In another large-sized mixing bowl, combine canned pumpkin, 1/2 cup of sugar, milk, 3 remaining eggs, ground mace, and pumpkin pie spice. Mix to combine well; then, pour this mixture over cake mixture in the baking dish.

In a food processor, combine 1/4 cup of margarine with 1/2 cup of sugar and reserved cake mix. Pulse until your mixture resembles coarse crumbs.

Spread over pumpkin mixture. Afterwards, sprinkle chopped pecans over all. Bake in the preheated oven about 50 minutes, till top of pumpkin cake is golden. Serve with a dollop of ice cream. Enjoy!

Fresh Berry Cheesecake

(Ready in about 30 minutes | Servings 12)

Ingredients

10 graham crackers

1 stick butter, melted

1 cup cream cheese, at room temperature

3/4 cup milk

1/4 cup brown sugar

1/2 teaspoon ground cinnamon

1/4 teaspoon anise seed

1 tablespoon fresh pineapple juice

1-pint fresh mixed berries

Directions

Begin by preheating an oven to 375 degrees F. Line your pan with a baking paper.

Grind crackers in a food processor. Add melted butter and mix to combine. Spread the mixture onto baking paper. Bake about 10 minutes; allow to cool completely.

In the meantime, mix together the cream cheese, milk, brown sugar, cinnamon, and anise seed. Add pineapple juice and stir until everything is well blended.

Spoon mixture onto prepared cooled crust. Spread fresh mixed berries over all. Serve chilled and enjoy!

Cranberry Chocolate Cookies

(Ready in about 35 minutes | Servings 10)

Ingredients

1 cup dried cranberries	1 cup sugar
2 tablespoons water	2 eggs, lightly beaten
1/3 cup cherry liquor	1 teaspoon cardamom
1 ½ cups flour	1 teaspoon pure vanilla extract
1/4 teaspoon kosher salt	1 ¼ cups chocolate chips
1/2 teaspoon baking powder	1/2 cup pecan, chopped
1 stick butter	

Directions

Start by preheating an oven to 375 degrees F. Then, coat your baking sheets with baking paper.

In a saucepan, place cranberries, water, cherry liqueur; bring to a boil. Remove the saucepan from the heat and allow to stand for 15 minutes. Drain cranberries and reserve.

Next, sift flour, kosher salt and baking powder in a medium bowl. Add butter, sugar, eggs, cardamom, and vanilla extract. Mix until everything is well blended.

Stir in cranberries, chocolate chips, and pecans. Mix again to combine.

Then, scoop tablespoons of dough onto prepared cookie sheets. Bake about 13 minutes. Transfer to a cooling rack before serving time. Serve.

Frozen Berry Delight

(Ready in about 15 minutes + chilling time | Servings 8)

Ingredients

2 cups low-fat cream cheese

1 box strawberry gelatin, sugar-free

1 tablespoon pure coconut extract

1 cup frozen raspberries

1 cup frozen strawberries

Coconut flakes, as garnish

Directions

Place all the above ingredients, except coconut flakes, in a bowl of a food processor.

Process until creamy, uniform, and smooth.

Pour into eight chilled dessert glasses. Serve chilled, sprinkle with coconut flakes, and enjoy!

Rich Caramel Cake

(Ready in about 25 minutes + chilling time | Servings 8)

Ingredients

2/3 cup butter, at room temperature

1/4 cup sugar

1 ¼ cups flour

1 stick butter

1/2 cup packed light brown sugar

1/2 cup condensed milk

2 tablespoons ground walnuts

1 ¼ cups chocolate chips

Directions

Begin by preheating an oven to 350 degrees F.

In a mixing bowl, combine together 2/3 cup butter, sugar, and flour. Press into a square baking pan and bake about 20 minutes.

To make the caramel layer: In a heavy skillet, combine 1 stick butter, light brown sugar, milk, and walnuts; bring to a boil over medium heat. Continue to boil for 5 minutes longer. Turn off the heat.

Beat vigorously with a spoon. Pour the mixture over baked crust.

Melt chocolate chips in a microwave-safe bowl for 1 minute. Drizzle the melted chocolate over the caramel layer. Serve chilled and enjoy!

Easiest and Yummiest Party Dessert

(Ready in about 20 minutes + chilling time | Servings 8)

Ingredients

40 small pretzels   40 whole pecans

40 pieces of chocolate candy

Directions

Preheat an oven to 250 degrees F.

Arrange the pretzel pieces on a cookie sheet. Top with chocolate candies.

Place in the oven for about 15 minutes

Place the pecans on top. Allow to cool completely before serving. Enjoy!

Old-Fashioned Cherry Meringues

(Ready in about 20 minutes | Servings 8)

Ingredients

2 large-sized egg whites

3/4 cup sugar

1/2 cup almonds, chopped

1/2 cup dried cherries

1/4 teaspoon grated nutmeg

1/4 teaspoon cardamom

1/2 teaspoon pure almond extract

1/2 cup shaved chocolate

Directions

Begin by preheating your oven to 350 degrees F. Then, line a cookie sheet with a foil.

Then, beat egg whites until stiff.

Gradually add sugar; mix to combine. Add the rest of the above ingredients. Drop the batter by teaspoons onto the cookie sheets.

Turn off the oven before putting your cookies in.

Leave them overnight.

Chocolate Jelly Cookies

(Ready in about 25 minutes | Servings 6)

Ingredients

1 stick butter

1 ¼ cups granulated sugar

1 medium-sized egg, lightly beaten

1 teaspoon almond extract

1/4 teaspoon ground cinnamon

1/4 teaspoon grated nutmeg

1/4 teaspoon cardamom

1 ½ cups fine pastry flour

1/2 cups cocoa powder

A pinch of salt

1/2 teaspoon baking soda

1/4 teaspoon baking powder

1 teaspoon orange juice

Orange jelly, as garnish

Directions

Begin by preheating an oven to 325 degrees F.

In a mixing bowl, cream the butter with granulated sugar until fluffy. Add the egg, almond extract, cinnamon, nutmeg, and cardamom.

In another mixing bowl, sift the flour, cocoa powder, salt, baking soda, and baking powder. Add the orange juice.

Add the flour mixture to the butter mixture. Shape the batter into 12 balls; make indentation in center of each cookie. Place orange jelly in the indentation.

Bake approximately 15 minutes. Serve at room temperature and enjoy!

Coconut Caramel Cookies

(Ready in about 25 minutes | Servings 6)

Ingredients

For the Cookies:

1 ¼ cups sugar

1/2 cup margarine

1 medium-sized egg, slightly beaten

1/2 teaspoon ground cinnamon

1/4 teaspoon cardamom

1 teaspoon hazelnut extract

1 ½ cups all-purpose flour

1/2 cup cocoa powder

3/4 teaspoon salt

1/4 teaspoon baking soda

1/4 teaspoon baking powder

For the Topping:

1 ¼ cups coconut, shredded

3/4 cups caramel syrup

3/4 cup walnuts, toasted and chopped

Directions

Start by preheating an oven to 325 degrees F.

In a mixing bowl, combine together sugar, margarine, egg, cinnamon, cardamom, and hazelnut extract.

In another bowl, combine together the rest of the cookie ingredients.

Then, combine together dry mixture and wet mixture; chill. Roll the dough into 12 equal balls. Gently press the cookies down with the bottom of a glass; make an indentation with finger.

In a separate bowl, combine together topping ingredients. Put the topping into the indentation.

Bake approximately 15 minutes. Serve at room temperature.

Walnut Pumpkin Cookies

(Ready in about 25 minutes | Servings 6)

Ingredients

For the Topping:

1/4 cup granulated sugar

1/4 cup cream cheese

1/2 cup pumpkin

1 teaspoon pumpkin pie spice mix

1/2 teaspoon pure almond extract

1/4 cup brown sugar

1/4 cup walnuts, finely chopped

For the Cookies:

1/2 cup butter, softened

1 large-sized egg

1 ¼ cups sugar

1/2 cup graham cracker crumbs

1/2 teaspoon ground cinnamon

1/4 teaspoon grated nutmeg

1/4 teaspoon ground cloves

1 ½ cups all-purpose flour

A pinch of salt

1/2 teaspoon baking powder

Directions

First of all, combine together the topping ingredients; set in a refrigerator.

In a small-sized mixing bowl, combine butter and egg; mix to combine well.

In another large-sized mixing bowl, combine the sugar, graham crackers, cinnamon, nutmeg, cloves, flour, salt, and baking powder.

Next, prepare the dough by mixing together wet ingredients and dry ingredients. Mix thoroughly until everything is well blended.

Roll the dough into 12 balls. Slightly press your cookies down; make the indentations with a finger or with a teaspoon.

Put 1 teaspoon of topping into each indentation. Bake in a preheated oven at 325 degrees for 12 to 15 minutes. Transfer to a cooling rack before serving. Then, replace to a serving platter and enjoy.

Fresh Apple and Pear Pie

(Ready in about 1 hour | Servings 6)

Ingredients

9-inch uncooked pie dough

3 apples, peeled, cored and sliced

4 pears, peeled, cored and sliced

1/4 cup fresh orange juice

1/2 stick butter, melted

1 cup sugar

1/4 cup flour

3 eggs

A pinch of salt

1 teaspoon almond extract

Cinnamon, as garnish

Directions

Preheat your oven to 350 degrees F. Place the pie dough in a pie plate; arrange apples and pears in a circle on the crust.

Drizzle the fruits with orange juice. In a medium-sized mixing bowl, combine butter, sugar, flour, eggs, a pinch of salt, and almond extract. Mix until everything is well combined.

Pour mixture over the fruits. Sprinkle with ground cinnamon.

Bake approximately 50 minutes or until golden. Transfer to a cooling rack before serving. Garnish with a dollop of whipped cream if desired.

Mom's Peach Cobbler

(Ready in about 40 minutes | Servings 6)

Ingredients

Non-stick cooking spray

1 cup brown sugar

1 cup all-purpose flour

1/2 teaspoon baking soda

1 teaspoon baking powder

1/4 teaspoon salt

1 teaspoon pure almond extract

3/4 cup milk

1 stick butter, melted

1 (29-ounce) can peaches, sliced and drained

1/4 teaspoon ground nutmeg

1/2 teaspoon ground cinnamon

Directions

Begin by preheating an oven to 400 degrees F. Grease a baking dish with non-stick cooking spray.

In a large-sized bowl, combine sugar, flour, baking soda, baking powder, salt, and pure almond extract. Pour in milk; add the butter. Mix until everything is well combined.

Pour mixture into greased baking dish. Arrange peaches on top; sprinkle with nutmeg and cinnamon.

Bake about 30 minutes or until the cake is golden brown. Allow to cool completely before slicing and serving. Enjoy!

Chocolate Marshmallow Rolls

(Ready in about 20 minutes | Servings 10)

Ingredients

2 cups chocolate chips

2 tablespoons butter, melted

1 medium-sized egg, beaten

3 cups miniature marshmallows

1 cup pecans, chopped

1/2 teaspoon ground cinnamon

1/4 teaspoon grated nutmeg

1/4 teaspoon cardamom

Confectioner's sugar

Directions

In a heavy skillet, melt chocolate and butter over low flame. Remove from heat; then, add beaten egg, and mix well to combine.

In another bowl, mix together miniature marshmallows, pecans, cinnamon, nutmeg, and cardamom.

Pour chocolate mixture over the marshmallow mixture; mix well to combine. Divide mixture into two pieces. Next, sprinkle waxed paper with confectioner's sugar; shape each half of the batter into a roll about 8 inches long.

Set in a fridge before serving. Cut into slices and serve chilled.

Creamy Summer Cake

(Ready in about 50 minutes | Servings 12)

Ingredients

1 package chocolate cake mix

1 package instant chocolate pudding

4 medium-sized eggs, lightly beaten

1 (8-ounce) container sour cream

1/2 cup coconut oil, softened

1/2 cup water

4 squares baking chocolate, chopped

1 cup whipped cream

Directions

Begin by preheating an oven to 350 degrees F. Lightly grease 2 round baking pans with non-stick cooking spray.

Beat chocolate cake mix, chocolate pudding, eggs, sour cream, coconut oil, and water with an electric mixer; beat until the mixture is well blended.

Stir in chocolate and mix to combine well. Pour the batter into baking pans.

Bake about 40 minutes or until a stick inserted in center comes out clean.

Place the cakes on wire racks to completely. Frost the cakes with whipped cream. Garnish with chopped nuts if desired. Serve chilled.

Caramel Fruit Bars

(Ready in about 50 minutes | Servings 18)

Ingredients

1 cup sugar

1 stick butter, softened

1/4 cup shortening

1 ½ cups quick-cooking oats

1 ¾ cups flour

1/4 teaspoon cardamom

1/2 teaspoon ground cinnamon

1/8 teaspoon salt

1/2 teaspoon baking powder

1/2 teaspoon baking soda

3 apples, peeled, cored and chopped

1/2 cup raisins

3 tablespoons flour

1 bag (14-ounce) caramels

Directions

Begin by preheating an oven to 400 degrees F. In a mixing bowl, combine together sugar, butter, and shortening.

Then, add the oats, 1 ¾ cups flour, cardamom, cinnamon, salt, baking powder, and baking soda. Reserve 2 cups of flour mixture; press remaining flour mixture in a baking dish.

Next, toss chopped apples and raisins with 3 tablespoons flour; spread over flour mixture in the baking dish.

In a small-sized skillet, heat caramels over low heat; stir until melted; pour the caramel mixture evenly over apples. Sprinkle with reserved flour mixture.

Bake about 30 minutes. Cut into 36 bars. Transfer to a serving platter and serve chilled.

Festive Pecan and Cherry Cake

(Ready in about 1 hour 20 minutes | Servings 12)

Ingredients

1 cup cream cheese, softened	2 ¼ cups all-purpose flour
2 sticks butter, softened	1/2 teaspoon baking soda
1 cup white sugar	1 teaspoon baking powder
1/2 cup brown sugar	1 cup candy cherries
1/2 teaspoon almond extract	1 cup pecans
1 teaspoon vanilla extract	1 ½ cups confectioner's sugar
3 large-sized eggs, lightly beaten	2 tablespoons milk

Directions

Begin by preheating an oven to 350 degrees F. Grease and flour a tube.

Using an electric mixer, combine cream cheese, butter, white sugar, brown sugar, almond extract, and vanilla together; mix until everything is well blended.

Gradually add the eggs and mix well to combine. Add 2 cups of flour, baking soda, and baking powder.

In a separate bowl, combine the remaining 1/4 cup of flour with the candy cherries and pecans; fold this mixture into the batter.

Bake in the preheated oven for 1 hour. Allow to cool for 15 minutes before removing from the pan.

Mix confectioner's sugar with milk for glaze. Glaze cake and serve.

Caramel Pear Cake

(Ready in about 50 minutes | Servings 12)

Ingredients

1/2 cup caramel topping

1/2 teaspoon anise seed

1/2 teaspoon ground cinnamon

6 large-sized pears, cored, peeled and chopped

2/3 cup flour

1/2 cup packed brown sugar

1 teaspoon lemon juice

1 stick butter, cold

2/3 cup quick-cooking oats

Directions

Start by preheating an oven to 375 degrees F.

In a large-sized mixing bowl, stir together caramel topping, anise seed, and cinnamon; mix until everything is well blended.

Add pears; toss to coat well. Spread the mixture in a baking dish.

In a bowl, mix together the flour, brown sugar, and lemon juice. Cut in butter and stir until the mixture looks like coarse crumbs. Stir in quick-cooking oats. Spread mixture over the pears in the baking dish.

Bake about 50 minutes till the top is golden brown. Serve with whipped cream if desired. Enjoy!

Coconut Cranberry Loaf Cakes

(Ready in about 1 hour | Servings 16)

Ingredients

1 pound margarine, softened

4 cups sugar

8 eggs

1/2 teaspoon baking soda

1/2 teaspoon baking powder

1 teaspoon pure coconut extract

1 teaspoon pure vanilla extract

3 tablespoons anise seeds

3/4 cup walnuts, chopped

8 cups flour

1 bag dried cranberries

1/2 cup coconut, shredded

Directions

Begin by preheating an oven to 350 degrees F.

In a mixing bowl, combine together margarine, sugar, eggs, baking soda, baking powder, coconut extract, pure vanilla extract, anise seed and walnuts; mix until everything is well combined.

Slowly and gradually add flour; stir to combine well. Stir in cranberries and coconut.

Divide your dough into four equal balls. Shape each ball into a loaf.

Then, bake loafs about 50 minutes on a baking sheet with sides. Transfer to a cooling rack. Serve.

Cherry Granola Bars

(Ready in about 1 hour | Servings 16)

Ingredients

1 cup chocolate, finely chopped

1/2 cup granola

1/4 cup dried cherries

1/2 teaspoon ground cinnamon

1/4 teaspoon cardamom

1/2 teaspoon pure almond extract

1/4 cup slivered almonds, lightly toasted

Directions

First of all, line the inside of an 8-inch square baking pan with foil.

Melt the chocolate in a microwave.

Spread melted chocolate in an even layer in the baking pan. Then, sprinkle with granola, cherries, cinnamon, cardamom, almond extract, and almonds. Set in a refrigerator until solid, or about 1 hour.

Store in an airtight container in the refrigerator.

Carrot Pineapple Cake

(Ready in about 35 minutes | Servings 8)

Ingredients

2 cups flour

1 teaspoon baking powder

1 teaspoon baking soda

1/8 teaspoon salt

1/2 teaspoon anise seed

1 teaspoon cardamom

1 teaspoon ground cinnamon

1 ¾ cups white sugar

1/2 cup coconut oil

3/4 cups applesauce

3 large-sized eggs

1/2 teaspoon almond extract

1 teaspoon vanilla extract

1 ½ cups carrots, shredded

1/2 cup peaches, diced

1 cup coconut, shredded

1 cup pecans, chopped

1 cup crushed pineapple

For the Frosting

1 cup cream cheese

1/4 cup butter, softened

1 teaspoon vanilla extract

2 cups confectioners' sugar

Directions

Begin by preheating an oven to 350 degrees F. Grease and flour round pans. Mix flour, baking powder, baking soda, salt, anise seed, cardamom, and cinnamon.

Make a well in the center and add sugar, oil, applesauce, eggs, almond and vanilla extract; mix to combine. Stir in carrots, peaches, coconut, pecans, and pineapple.

Divide the batter among baking pans. Bake for about 25 minutes. Allow to cool on a wire rack.

To make the frosting: Beat the cream cheese, butter and vanilla until everything is well blended.

Then, add the confectioners' sugar and beat until the mixture is creamy.

Frost your cake and serve chilled.

Chilled Nutty Cookies

(Ready in about 25 minutes | Servings 20)

Ingredients

2/3 cup flaked coconut

1/4 cup honey

1/3 cup nut butter

1/4 cup corn syrup

1/4 cup chocolate chips

2 tablespoons cocoa

1/2 teaspoon allspice

2 tablespoons ground walnuts

3 cups corn flakes, lightly crushed

Directions

Coat a baking sheet with parchment paper or a silicone mat.

Heat a cast-iron skillet over medium-high flame. Toast the flaked coconut about 4 minutes. Transfer toasted coconut to a bowl and set aside.

In a medium-sized saucepan over medium heat, combine honey, nut butter, and corn syrup. Bring mixture to a boil, stirring frequently. Turn off the heat and add chocolate chips, cocoa, allspice, and walnuts.

Stir until chocolate chips have melted completely. Then, add corn flakes and reserved toasted coconut.

Drop by tablespoonful onto baking sheet; refrigerate at least 15 minutes. Serve.

Refreshing Lemon Pudding Treats

(Ready in about 45 minutes | Servings 6)

Ingredients

Non-stick cooking spray

3 large-sized eggs, separated into yolks and whites

2 tablespoons coconut oil

1 cup milk

4 tablespoons fresh lemon juice

3/4 cup sugar

1 tablespoon molasses

1/2 teaspoon ground cinnamon

1/2 teaspoon ground cloves

1/3 cup flour

1/8 teaspoon salt

Directions

Begin by preheating an oven to 350 degrees F. Oil 6 ramekins with non-stick cooking spray; place them on a large baking pan.

In a medium-sized bowl, whisk egg yolks and coconut oil until smooth. Pour in milk and lemon juice. Stir in sugar, molasses, cinnamon, cloves, flour; mix to combine.

In a separate mixing bowl, beat the egg whites and salt using an electric mixer on high speed. To make the batter: Gently add egg whites into egg yolk mixture.

Pour the batter into prepared ramekins. Pour hot tap water into a baking pan.

Bake about 35 minutes. Allow to cool completely before serving.

Cherry Rum Bread Pudding

(Ready in about 1 hour + chilling time | Servings 8)

Ingredients

For the Sauce:

2 cups whole milk

6 egg yolks, lightly beaten

1/3 cup sugar

1 teaspoon pure vanilla extract

3 tablespoons dark rum

For the Pudding:

12 slices cinnamon swirl bread

4 tablespoons butter, softened

1/2 cup dried cherries

4 large-sized eggs

2 cups milk

1/2 cup heavy cream

1/2 teaspoon pure almond extract

1 teaspoon pure vanilla extract

1/2 cup sugar

Directions

To prepare the sauce: In a saucepan, bring milk to a simmer over medium-high flame.

In a large-sized mixing bowl, whisk yolks and sugar until the mixture has thickened.

Gradually pour in hot milk. Return the mixture back to the saucepan; cook about 10 minutes over low flame.

Transfer to a bowl; stir in vanilla extract and rum. Cover and chill at least 2 hours.

To make the pudding: Preheat your oven to 350 degrees F; grease a baking dish.

Treat each bread slice with softened butter. Cut bread into bite-sized chunks; transfer the bread chunks to the baking dish and sprinkle them with dried cherries.

In a mixing bowl, combine the rest of the ingredients. Pour the mixture over bread in the baking dish. Bake approximately 55 minutes.

Divide among 8 dessert dishes; serve with reserved chilled sauce. Sprinkle with some extra dried cherries, if desired.

Everyday Chocolate Pudding

(Ready in about 15 minutes | Servings 8)

Ingredients

1/4 cup sugar

3 tablespoons corn flour

2 ½ cups milk

1 cup chocolate, chopped

1/2 teaspoon allspice

1/2 tablespoon butter

1/4 teaspoon grated nutmeg

1 teaspoon pure vanilla extract

Chocolate sprinkles, as garnish

Chopped nuts, as garnish

Directions

In a medium-sized skillet, combine together sugar and corn flour. Slowly and gradually add 1/2 cup of milk, whisking constantly. Then, whisk in remaining 2 cups of milk.

Increase heat to medium-high, bringing the mixture to a boil. Then, lower heat to medium and cook an additional 4 minutes, or until the mixture is thickened.

Remove from heat; stir in the chocolate chips, allspice, butter, nutmeg, and vanilla extract. Whisk until the mixture is smooth.

Divide the chocolate pudding among 8 parfait glasses. Serve warm or chilled, garnished with chocolate sprinkles and chopped nuts. Enjoy!

Yummiest Banana Pudding Ever

(Ready in about 15 minutes + chilling time | Servings 6)

Ingredients

1 tablespoon cornstarch

1/3 cup sugar

1 ½ cups half-and-half

2 large egg yolks

1 tablespoon butter

1/4 teaspoon grated nutmeg

1/2 teaspoon ground cinnamon

1/2 teaspoon anise seed

2 teaspoons pure coconut extract

4 ripe bananas, sliced

Vanilla wafer crumbs, as garnish

Directions

Combine the cornstarch and sugar together in a saucepan. Gradually whisk in half-and-half; then, gradually add egg yolks. Continue cooking, whisking often, 3 to 5 minutes or until pudding thickens.

Remove from heat; add butter, grated nutmeg, ground cinnamon, anise seed and coconut extract; whisk to combine well. Transfer to a 2-cup measuring cup that has a pouring spout.

Place banana slices on the bottom of custard cups. Pour the pudding over banana slices.

Set in a refrigerator at least 2 hours. Top with vanilla wafer crumbs and serve.

Vanilla Cherry Rice Pudding

(Ready in about 40 minutes + chilling time | Servings 6)

Ingredients

1 ½ cups water

1 vanilla bean

1 cinnamon stick

2/3 cup rice

2 ½ cups milk

3 chai-spice tea bags

1/2 cup dried cherries

2 eggs

1/2 cup sugar

1 ½ teaspoons vanilla extract

1/2 cup heavy cream

Directions

Place water, vanilla bean, cinnamon stick, and rice in a saucepan over medium-high heat. Bring to a boil; then, reduce heat to low.

Cook about 10 minutes. Discard vanilla and cinnamon and reserve.

In a separate pan, warm milk and add tea bags. After 10 minutes, remove tea bags. Add reserved rice and dried cherries; simmer for about 10 minutes.

In a bowl, mix together the eggs and sugar. Slowly add the egg mixture to the milk mixture, whisking constantly. Cook 2 to 3 minutes. Remove from heat and add vanilla extract. Set in a refrigerator at least 1 hour.

Whip cream until soft peaks form with an electric mixer. Gently fold in whipped cream.

Spoon into dessert bowls. Serve chilled and enjoy.

Overnight Berry and Oat Dessert

(Ready in about 10 minutes | Servings 1)

Ingredients

1 cup oats

1/2 cup whole milk

2 tablespoons flavored yoghurt

1/2 cup mixed berries

Chopped nuts, as garnish

Directions

Put the oats into a bowl.

Pour in the milk and yogurt. Mix until the oats are soaked well.

Add mixed berries; mix until everything is well blended.

Set in a fridge overnight. Sprinkle with chopped nuts and serve chilled.

Cranberry Pineapple Dessert Salad

(Ready in about 10 minutes | Servings 6)

Ingredients

1 (16-ounce) can whole cranberry sauce

2 (20-ounce) cans pineapple tidbits, drained

2 oranges, chopped

1/2 cup almonds, chopped

2 cups miniature marshmallows

1 (8-ounce) package whipped topping

Directions

In a large-sized mixing bowl, combine together cranberry sauce, pineapple, oranges, almonds, and miniature marshmallows.

Next, fold in whipped topping.

Set in a refrigerator. Divide among six dessert bowls and serve chilled. Enjoy!

Chocolate Pecan Cookies

(Ready in about 15 minutes | Servings 12)

Ingredients

2 cups sugar substitute

1/2 cup butter

1/2 cup almond milk

3/4 cup pecans, chopped

3 cups quick-cooking oats

1 cup chocolate, chopped

1/2 teaspoon allspice

1 teaspoon pure almond extract

1/2 teaspoon pure vanilla extract

Directions

In a saucepan, combine together sugar, butter, and almond milk. Bring to a boil for 1 minute.

Remove the pan from the heat. Add the rest of the ingredients. Mix to combine.

Drop by teaspoonful on wax paper. Serve.

Walnut Chocolate Fudge

(Ready in about 35 minutes | Servings 4)

Ingredients

1/2 cup cocoa powder

1 pound powdered sugar

1 stick butter

1/4 cup whole milk

1/2 teaspoon hazelnut extract

1 teaspoon pure vanilla extract

1/2 cup walnuts, chopped

Directions

Put all ingredients, excluding hazelnut extract, vanilla and walnuts, into a microwavable bowl.

Microwave for 1 minute 30 seconds. Mix until everything is well combined.

Then, add hazelnut extract, vanilla, extract, and walnuts. Stir to combine.

Line a glass pan with wax paper. Pour the mixture into the pan and place it in a refrigerator until set.

Flavorful Chocolate Nutty Balls

(Ready in about 15 minutes | Servings 6)

Ingredients

1/4 cup coconut, shredded

1/4 cup cashews, chopped

1/4 cup almonds, chopped

2 tablespoons peanut butter

2 tablespoons vanilla protein powder

3 tablespoons tahini

1 tablespoon raw cacao powder

4 tablespoons chocolate syrup

Directions

To make the batter: Place all the above ingredients in a large-sized mixing bowl. Mix to combine.

Shape the batter into small-sized balls. Set in a refrigerator before serving.

Best Coconut Pie Ever

(Ready in about 15 minutes + chilling time | Servings 8)

Ingredients

2 boxes (3.4 ounces) instant cream pudding mix

2 cups whole milk

2/3 cup coconut, shredded

1/4 teaspoon anise seed

1 teaspoon pure vanilla extract

1/2 teaspoon pure coconut extract

1 cup whipped cream

1 prepared graham cracker pie crust

Directions

In a large-sized mixing bowl, combine together the pudding mix and milk for about 2 minutes.

Stir in coconut, anise seed, vanilla extract, and coconut extract. Fold in 3/4 of the whipped cream. Mix until everything is well combined

Pour the mixture into the prepared graham cracker pie crust.

Afterwards, top with remaining whipped cream. Set in a refrigerator before slicing and serving. Serve chilled and enjoy.

Creamy Lemon Cake

(Ready in about 50 minutes + chilling time | Servings 4)

Ingredients

1 ⅓ cups flour	1 ¼ cup sugar
1/2 cup sugar	1/4 teaspoon ground cloves
3/4 cup butter	1/2 teaspoon anise seed
For the Filling:	A pinch of salt
4 large egg yolks	3/4 cup fresh lemon juice
4 eggs	3 tablespoons butter

Directions

Begin by preheating an oven to 350 degrees F. Line a baking pan with a foil.

To prepare the dough: In a medium-sized mixing bowl, sift the flour and sugar; stir to combine well. Cut in the butter and stir until your mixture resembles coarse crumbs.

Press the dough into the bottom of the baking pan. Bake your crust approximately 20 minutes.

Meanwhile, prepare the filling. In a medium-sized pot, over medium heat, whisk the egg yolks, eggs, sugar, cloves, anise seed, and salt. Then, add the lemon juice and butter.

Cook for about 10 minutes; make sure to stir constantly. Pour the filling over the crust. Next, bake for about 20 minutes.

Allow to cool on a wire rack Then, replace to a refrigerator for at least 2 hours. Cut the cake into squares, arrange them on a serving platter and serve.

Coconut Bread Pudding

(Ready in about 1 hour 15 minutes | Servings 12)

Ingredients

6 slices bread, torn into bite-sized pieces

2 tablespoons coconut oil, melted

1/2 cup dates, chopped

2 cups whole milk

4 eggs, beaten

3/4 cup sugar

1/2 teaspoon grated cardamom

1/2 teaspoon ground cloves

1 teaspoon ground cinnamon

1 teaspoon pure coconut extract

Flaked coconut for garnish (optional)

Directions

Begin by preheating your oven to 350 degrees F. Lightly grease 8-inch square baking pan with non-stick cooking spray or melted butter.

Arrange the bread pieces in your baking pan. Drizzle coconut oil over bread. Sprinkle with chopped dates.

In a mixing bowl, combine milk, eggs, sugar, cardamom, cloves, cinnamon, and coconut extract. Beat until everything is well mixed.

Pour this milk mixture over the bread pieces; lightly push down the bread pieces in order to soak up the milk mixture.

Bake for 45 minutes; divide among 12 dessert bowls and serve at room temperature. Sprinkle with flaked coconut, if used. Enjoy!

Bourbon Bread Pudding

(Ready in about 1 hour 10 minutes | Servings 10)

Ingredients

For the Pudding

1 loaf bread, at least a day old,

3 eggs, well beaten

4 cups milk

1 cup brown sugar

1 cup white sugar

1 teaspoon pure almond extract

1 teaspoon pure vanilla extract

1 cup raisins, soaked

1/2 teaspoon cinnamon

For the Sauce:

1 stick butter, melted

1 egg, lightly beaten

1 cup bourbon

1 cup sugar

Directions

Begin by preheating an oven to 350 degrees F.

Tear the bread loaf into small pieces. Replace to the greased square baking pan.

In a mixing bowl, combine together the rest of the pudding ingredients. Pour over the bread pieces. Then, push down with a fork.

Bake about 45 minutes in the preheated oven.

Meanwhile, add 1 stick of butter to the medium-sized saucepan. Melt the butter over medium-low heat.

Then, slowly add the rest of the sauce ingredients, whisking to blend well. Cook until the sauce is creamy and soft.

Afterwards, serve your bread pudding with bourbon sauce on the side. Enjoy!

Family Favorite Banana Bread Pudding

(Ready in about 2 hours 10 minutes | Servings 8)

Ingredients

1 loaf day-old French bread, torn into pieces

4 cups whole milk

3 eggs, lightly beaten

1 cup granulated sugar

1 tablespoon pure vanilla extract

4 medium-sized ripe bananas, mashed

1/2 cup dried apricots, chopped

1 cup dried dates, chopped

1 teaspoon freshly grated nutmeg

1/2 teaspoon allspice

1 teaspoon cinnamon

Whipped cream as garnish

Directions

Start by preheating an oven to 325 degrees F. Oil a square casserole baking dish.

In a large-sized bowl, place the bread pieces and milk; let soak for 1 hour.

In a separate bowl, combine together eggs, sugar, and pure vanilla extract. Beat until the mixture is frothy and smooth. Pour over the bread mixture.

Fold in the bananas, apricots, dates, nutmeg, allspice, and cinnamon. Gently stir to combine.

Bake about 1 hour and 10 minutes in the center of your oven. Serve at room temperature with whipped cream, if desired. Enjoy!

Kid-Friendly Chocolate Pudding

(Ready in about 1 hour 20 minutes | Servings 6)

Ingredients

4 cups day-old bread cubes

1 ¾ cups whipping cream

1/2 cup sugar

1/4 cup whole milk

1 cup chocolate

1 large-sized egg

1/4 teaspoon grated nutmeg

A pinch of salt

2 tablespoons granulated sugar

Directions

Begin by preheating an oven to 325 degrees F. Lightly oil a shallow baking dish with cooking spray. Arrange the bread cubes in the baking dish.

Add whipping cream, sugar, and whole milk to a saucepan; cook over medium heat bringing to a simmer; cook until sugar dissolves.

Next, turn off the heat; add the chocolate and stir to combine well. Set aside keeping hot.

In a large-sized mixing bowl, beat the egg with grated nutmeg and salt until creamy. Then, whisk the chocolate mixture into the egg mixture.

Pour prepared mixture into prepared baking dish; sprinkle with 2 tablespoons of granulated sugar.

Bake until the custard thickens, or approximately 50 minutes. Divide among serving dishes and serve warm. Add decorative sprinkles or chocolate shavings on top if desired.

Easy Cheesy Dessert

(Ready in about 2 hours 20 minutes | Servings 8)

Ingredients

1 ¼ cups cream cheese, room temperature

1⁄2 cup margarine, softened

1 teaspoon pure almond extract

A pinch of salt

1-2 drops of rum

3⁄4 cup sugar

2 tablespoons granulated sugar

3⁄4 cup chocolate chips

1/2 cup walnuts, chopped

Directions

In a bowl, beat together cream cheese, margarine, almond extract, salt, and the drops of rum; beat until your mixture is fluffy.

Gradually add sugars and continue to beat until everything is well combined. Then, stir in chocolate chips.

Then, refrigerate at least 2 hours.

Sprinkle with chopped walnuts (raw or toasted) and serve.

Amazing Berry Treat

(Ready in about 1 hour 15 minutes | Servings 6)

Ingredients

1 cup blackberries

1 cup blueberries

Juice of 1/2 lemon

1/2 teaspoon ground cinnamon

1/2 teaspoon grated nutmeg

3/4 cup sugar

3 tablespoons butter

1 cup all-purpose flour

1/2 teaspoon baking soda

1 teaspoon baking powder

1/4 teaspoon sea salt

1/2 cup whole milk

For the Topping:

1/2 cup sugar

1 tablespoon cornstarch

1 cup boiling water

Directions

Arrange blackberries and blueberries at the bottom of a large-sized dessert bowl. Drizzle with lemon juice.

Then, sprinkle with cinnamon and nutmeg. Beat together the sugar and butter until creamy. Add flour, baking soda, baking powder, salt, and milk. Mix until everything is well combined.

Spread the mixture over the berries.

To make the topping: Combine together sugar and cornstarch. Spread this mixture over the batter. Slowly pour boiling water over the dessert.

Preheat an oven to 350 degrees F. Bake your dessert about 1 hour.

Summer Fruit Dessert

(Ready in about 1 hour 15 minutes | Servings 6)

Ingredients

1 cup apricots, cubed

1 cup peaches, cubed

Juice of 1/2 lemon

1/2 teaspoon allspice

1/4 teaspoon ground cloves

1/2 teaspoon grated nutmeg

3/4 cup sugar

3 tablespoons margarine or butter, softened

1 cup all-purpose flour

1 teaspoon baking powder

A pinch of salt

1/2 cup whole milk

For the Topping:

1/2 cup sugar

1/2 teaspoon vanilla extract

1/2 teaspoon cinnamon

1 tablespoon cornstarch

1 cup boiling water

Directions

Begin by preheating an oven to 350 degrees F

Arrange apricots and peaches at the bottom of your dessert bowl. Drizzle with fresh lemon juice.

Then, sprinkle with allspice, cloves, and nutmeg. Mix together the sugar and margarine (or butter) until creamy. Stir in the flour, baking powder, salt, and whole milk. Mix until everything is well incorporated.

Spread the mixture over the fruits in the bowl.

To make the topping: Mix together sugar, vanilla, cinnamon, and cornstarch. Spread the sugar mixture over the batter. Afterwards, pour boiling water over your dessert in the bowl.

Bake about 1 hour. Serve with ice cream, if desired.

Rich and Creamy Lemon Dessert

(Ready in about 2 hours 25 minutes | Servings 8)

Ingredients

1 stick butter, melted

1 cup all-purpose flour

1/2 teaspoon ground cinnamon

1 teaspoon pure coconut extract

2 cups sugar

A pinch of salt

2 cups cream cheese, softened

1 cup whipped cream

2 (3.5-ounce) packages instant lemon pudding

3 cups milk

Directions

Begin by preheating your oven to 350 degrees F. Then, prepare a suitable baking dish.

In a large-sized mixing bowl, combine together the butter, flour, cinnamon, and coconut extract. Mix to combine; then add to the baking dish.

Bake about 20 minutes. Then, set aside to cool.

Combine the sugar, salt, cheese and whipped cream until well mixed. Spread the mixture over crust.

Mix lemon pudding with milk. Spread the pudding mixture over cream cheese mixture. Serve chilled and enjoy!

Lush Creamy Chocolate Treat

(Ready in about 2 hours 25 minutes | Servings 8)

Ingredients

Non-stick cooking spray

1 cup flour

1 stick butter, melted

1 teaspoon pure vanilla extract

1 cup powdered sugar

1 cup sugar

2 cups cream cheese, softened

1 cup whipped cream

2 packages instant chocolate pudding

3 cups milk

Directions

Start by preheating your oven to 350 degrees F. Lightly grease a square baking pan with non-stick cooking spray.

In a mixing bowl, mix together the flour, butter, and vanilla extract. Mix until everything is well combined; then add the mixture to the baking pan.

Bake about 20 minutes. Allow to cool completely.

Mix the powdered sugar, sugar, cream cheese and whipped cream until everything is well combined. Spread the mixture over reserved cooled crust.

Then, combine together the chocolate pudding and milk. Spread the chocolate mixture over the cream mixture. Serve chilled!

Everyday Almond-Apple Pie

(Ready in about 50 minutes | Servings 12)

Ingredients

1 yellow cake mix

1 egg

1/3 cup margarine, softened

For the Topping:

1 (21-ounce) can apple pie filling

1/2 cup sugar

1/2 cup almonds, chopped

1/2 teaspoon grated nutmeg

1 teaspoon ground cinnamon

1 cup sour cream

1 egg

1 teaspoon pure almond extract

Directions

Begin by preheating an oven to 350 degrees F.

In a bowl, combine yellow cake mix, egg, and margarine; beat with an electric mixer on low speed until the mixture is crumbly.

Press the mixture into a baking pan. Spread the apple pie filling over the top.

In another bowl, combine together the sugar, almonds, nutmeg, and ground cinnamon. Sprinkle the mixture over apple pie filling.

In a small-sized mixing bowl, blend sour cream with egg and almond extract. Top the cake with this cream mixture.

Bake approximately 40 minutes and serve at room temperature.

Superfast Fruit Bars

(Ready in about 35 minutes | Servings 12)

Ingredients

2 (20-ounce) packages sugar cookie dough

1 (21-ounce) can blueberry pie filling

1/4 teaspoon ground cloves

1/4 teaspoon allspice

2 teaspoons granulated sugar

Directions

Begin by preheating your oven to 425 degrees F. Then, press one roll of cookie dough into a baking pan.

Next, spread blueberry pie filling over prepared dough. Scatter remaining pieces of cookie dough over the filling.

Sprinkle with cloves, allspice, and granulated sugar. Bake about 15 minutes; cut into bars and serve.

Easiest and Funniest Chocolate Dessert

(Ready in about 10 minutes | Servings 6)

Ingredients

1 cup cream cheese

1 cup heavy cream

1 cup water, cold

1 (1-ounce) package instant chocolate pudding mix

Chocolate shavings, as garnish

Directions

Beat all the above ingredients together, excluding the chocolate shavings.

Divide among 6 dessert cups. Sprinkle with chocolate shavings and serve chilled.

French Fruit Clafouti

(Ready in about 1 hour | Servings 6)

Ingredients

1 cup flour

1/2 cup sugar

1/2 teaspoon baking soda

1 teaspoon baking powder

1/4 teaspoon salt

3 tablespoons whole milk

3 eggs, lightly beaten

1 teaspoon pure almond extract

2 ½ ounces butter, softened

1 pound apples, peeled and cubed

1 pound pears, peeled and cubed

Directions

Begin by preheating an oven to 450 degrees F. Butter a round cake tin.

In a large-sized bowl, sift the flour, sugar, baking soda, baking powder, and salt.

Make a well in the center of dry mixture; add the milk, eggs, and pure almond extract. Mix to combine.

Add the butter; then, mix to combine well in order to form a smooth batter. Fold in the apples and pears.

Bake about 30 minutes or until a wooden stick inserted in the center comes out clean. Next, turn out onto a wire rack in order to cool slightly. Serve and enjoy.

Bread Pudding with Ice Cream

(Ready in about 1 hour 40 minutes | Servings 6)

Ingredients

1 cup French bread, torn into pieces

8 tablespoons butter

1 cup pecans, chopped

1 cup semisweet chocolate chunks

4 eggs

1 cup sugar

1/2 cup cocoa powder

2 cups chocolate milk

1/2 teaspoon grated nutmeg

1/2 teaspoon ground cinnamon

1 teaspoon almond extract

1 teaspoon vanilla extract

Ice cream, as garnish

Directions

Begin by preheating an oven to 350 degrees F. Butter a baking dish and set aside.

Toss the bread pieces with the melted butter, pecans, and chocolate chunks. Spread the mixture in a baking dish.

In a mixing bowl, beat the eggs, sugar, cocoa powder, chocolate milk, nutmeg, cinnamon, almond extract, and vanilla extract.

Pour the mixture over the bread pieces in the baking dish. Let it soak for 30 minutes; push the bread down occasionally.

Bake until the pudding is just set or for about 40 minutes. Top with your favorite ice cream and serve warm!

Halloween Lush Nutty Dessert

(Ready in about 1 hour 15 minutes | Servings 12)

Ingredients

1 (16-ounce) can pumpkin

1 (5-ounce) can milk

1 cup sugar

1/4 teaspoon grated nutmeg

1/2 teaspoon ground cloves

1/2 teaspoon cinnamon

1 (18-ounce) dry cake mix

2 cups walnuts or almonds, chopped

2 sticks butter, melted

1 teaspoon pure vanilla extract

1 teaspoon pure almond extract

For the Topping:

1 (8-ounce) package cream cheese

1 cup powdered sugar

2 cups whipped cream

Directions

Preheat your oven to 350 degrees F.

Mix the pumpkin, milk, sugar, nutmeg, cloves, and cinnamon together; blend well.

Spread this mixture in a well-greased baking dish.

Sprinkle the cake mix over the pumpkin mix; make sure to break up any clumps.

Spread 1 cup of chopped nuts over the pumpkin mixture; top with melted butter, vanilla extract, and almond extract.

Bake approximately 1 hour or until the top is a golden brown. Allow to cool completely. Scatter remaining 1 cup of nuts on the top.

In the meantime, prepare the topping. In a bowl, combine together cream cheese and powdered sugar; add whipped cream and beat until the ingredients are well incorporated.

Spread the topping over the cooled cake. Serve and enjoy!

Yummy Peach and Banana Cobbler

(Ready in about 45 minutes | Servings 4)

Ingredients

1/2 cup all-purpose flour

1/2 cup sugar

1/2 cup milk

1/2 teaspoon baking soda

1 teaspoon baking powder

A pinch of sea salt

1 cup peaches, pitted and diced

1 cup banana, sliced

Directions

Start by preheating an oven to 350 degrees F.

Combine all of the above ingredients, except the peaches and bananas, in a large-sized bowl.

Pour the mixture into greased baking pan. Top with the peaches and bananas.

Bake approximately 40 minutes. Serve at room temperature with whipped cream if desired.

Simply Amazing Berry Cobbler

(Ready in about 45 minutes | Servings 4)

Ingredients

1/2 cup flour

1/2 cup sugar

1/2 cup whole milk

1 teaspoon pure vanilla extract

1 teaspoon baking powder

1 tablespoon fresh orange juice

1 cup raspberries, pitted and diced

1 cup blueberries, sliced

Directions

Begin by preheating an oven to 350 degrees F.

Combine all of the above ingredients, except the berries, in a bowl.

Pour this mixture into the baking pan. Top with the raspberries and blueberries.

Bake 40 to 45 minutes. Serve at room temperature and enjoy.

Lemon Meringue Pie

(Ready in about 15 minutes | Servings 4)

Ingredients

1 1/3 cups sugar

A pinch of kosher salt

1/2 cup corn flour

1 ½ cups water

3 egg yolks

Juice of 1 large-sized lemon

1/2 teaspoon grated nutmeg

1 teaspoon grated ginger

2 tablespoons butter

1 pie crust, prepared and baked

For the Meringue:

3 egg whites

6 tablespoons sugar

Directions

In a microwavable bowl, add sugar, salt, corn flour, and water. Stir to combine

Then, microwave on high for 5 minutes. Add the egg yolks, lemon, nutmeg, and ginger.

Microwave 3 minutes more. Add butter to the hot mixture and stir to combine well. Pour the mixture into pie crust. Allow to cool completely.

In a food processor, mix together the egg whites and sugar. Bake in a preheated oven at 350 degrees F about 5 minutes or until golden. Serve and enjoy!

Pillowy Coconut Custard Pie

(Ready in about 1 hour 10 minutes | Servings 8)

Ingredients

4 medium-sized eggs, lightly beaten

1 teaspoon pure vanilla extract

6 tablespoons butter

3⁄4 cup sugar

1⁄2 cup flour

1 cup coconut, shredded

2 cups milk

Directions

Begin by preheating an oven to 350 degrees F. Then, butter a pie plate and dust it with the flour.

Add all the above ingredients, except the coconut, to your blender or a food processor. Mix until everything is well blended.

Next, add the coconut and process until the mixture is creamy and uniform.

Pour the batter into the prepared pie plate; bake for 55 to 60 minutes. Cut into wedges and enjoy!

Everyday Family Fudge

(Ready in about 2 hours 10 minutes | Servings 8)

Ingredients

3 cups chocolate chips

14 ounces milk

2 tablespoons coffee

1 teaspoon pure vanilla extract

1/4 teaspoon grated nutmeg

1 teaspoon ground cinnamon

A pinch of salt

Directions

Line a baking pan with a foil and grease it with a butter.

Put all the above ingredients into a microwavable bowl; stir to combine and cook on high for about 1 minute.

Next, cover and refrigerate at least 2 hours.

Store in an airtight container.

Evergreen Pudding with Raisins

(Ready in about 35 minutes | Servings 6)

Ingredients

1 cup flour

1/3 cup sugar

2 tablespoons butter, soften

1 tablespoon baking soda

1 teaspoon baking powder

1/3 cup raisins

1/2 cup milk

1 3/4 cups warm water

1/4 teaspoon grated nutmeg

1/2 teaspoon cinnamon

1 teaspoon almond extract

2/3 cup sugar

Directions

Place flour, sugar, butter, baking soda, baking powder and raisins in a mixing bowl. Mix to combine. Add milk and mix again.

Pour the mixture into a baking dish.

In a bowl, combine the remaining ingredients. Pour the mixture over the dough in the baking dish.

Bake in the preheated oven at 350 degrees F, for about 30 minutes. Serve warm and enjoy.

Rum Caramel Bars

(Ready in about 55 minutes | Servings 20)

Ingredients

1 stick butter

1 ¼ cups sugar

2 eggs

A few drops of rum

2 teaspoons vanilla extract

1 ¼ cups flour

2 candy bars, chopped

2 tablespoons caramel sauce

Directions

Preheat your oven to 325 degrees F. Butter a square baking pan.

In a bowl, combine together the butter and brown sugar until the mixture is well combined. Then, add the eggs, one at a time.

Add rum and vanilla extract and mix to combine.

In a separate mixing bowl, mix flour and candy bars. Add the mixture to the butter mixture; mix to combine well.

Pour the mixture into the buttered baking pan and bake for about 40 minutes.

Afterwards, spread the caramel sauce over the hot cake. Serve at room temperature or chilled.

p.Cashew Mud Cake

(Ready in about 55 minutes | Servings 20)

Ingredients

1 cup cashews, chopped

2 packages fudge brownie mix

2 eggs

1/2 cup coconut oil

1/4 cup water

1 (10.5-ounce) bag miniature marshmallows

Chocolate frosting

Directions

Place the cashews in a single layer on a baking sheet. Bake at 350 degrees F for about 10 minutes.

Combine the brownie mix, eggs, coconut oil and water in a mixing bowl. Then, pour it into a greased pan.

Bake at 350 degrees F for about 25 minutes. Next, top with miniature marshmallows; bake 10 minutes longer.

Drizzle warm cake with your favorite chocolate frosting; sprinkle with toasted cashews. Serve.

Hot Swirl Cake

(Ready in about 35 minutes | Servings 8)

Ingredients

1 ½ cups flour

2 packages fast rise yeast

1/2 teaspoon ground cinnamon

1/4 teaspoon allspice

2 tablespoons granulated sugar

A pinch of salt

3⁄4 cup warm water

2 tablespoons coconut oil, softened

1 cup hot fudge sauce

1 cup powdered sugar

2 tablespoons milk

Directions

Grease a pie pan with non-stick cooking spray.

In the pan, combine together the flour, yeast, cinnamon, allspice, granulated sugar, salt, water, and coconut oil.

Top the batter with spoonfuls of the fudge sauce. Then, swirl fudge sauce into the batter with a spoon.

Bake in an oven at 350 degrees F for about 30 minutes, until it's firm in the center.

In a small-sized bowl, combine powdered sugar and milk; drizzle the mixture over warm cake. Serve.

Apricot Rice Pudding

(Ready in about 50 minutes | Servings 4)

Ingredients

1 ½ cups water

3⁄4 cup white rice

2 cups milk

1⁄3 cup sugar

1 egg, beaten

2⁄3 cup dried apricots, chopped

1 tablespoon butter

1⁄2 teaspoon coconut extract

Shredded coconut, as garnish (optional)

Directions

In a medium-sized pan, bring water to a boil. Add rice and simmer for 20 minutes until it is cooked.

In a separate saucepan, combine the cooked rice with 1 ½ cups of milk and sugar. Allow to cook over medium heat about 20 minutes.

Pour in remaining 1/2 cup milk, egg, and dried apricots. Continue cooking for 2 more minutes, stirring constantly.

Remove from the heat; stir in the butter and coconut extract. Divide among dessert bowls; sprinkle with coconut if used; serve warm.

Quick and Easy Cherry Delight

(Ready in about 20 minutes | Servings 4)

Ingredients

1/2 cup sugar

1 tablespoon corn flour

1/2 teaspoon ground cinnamon

4 cups cherries, pitted

1 cup shortbread cookies, crumbled

2 tablespoons butter, melted

1/4 cup pecans, toasted and chopped

Whipped cream, as garnish (optional)

Directions

In a small-sized mixing bowl, combine together the sugar, corn flour, and cinnamon. Transfer the mixture to a saucepan and add cherries.

Cook over medium heat, stirring occasionally; cook until the mixture is thickened and bubbly or for about 12 minutes.

Meanwhile, in a separate bowl, thoroughly combine shortbread cookies, butter, and pecans.

Afterwards, divide cherry mixture among four dessert bowls. Sprinkle with cookie mixture. Serve with whipped cream, if desired. Enjoy!

Chocolate and Hazelnut Parfaits

(Ready in about 20 minutes | Servings 4)

Ingredients

1 (4-serving-size) package chocolate instant pudding mix

2 cups whole milk

1/2 cup whipped dessert topping

1/4 cup hazelnuts, chopped

Chocolate curls, as garnish

Directions

Begin by preparing the pudding mix with milk according to package instructions.

Reserve 3/4 cup of the prepared pudding; fold in whipped dessert topping and mix until everything is well combined.

Divide remaining chocolate pudding among four dessert glasses. Top with chocolate and dessert topping mixture.

Sprinkle with hazelnuts and chocolate curls. Enjoy!

Healthy Berry and Yogurt Parfaits

(Ready in about 20 minutes | Servings 4)

Ingredients

3 cups flavored yogurt

1 cup raspberries

1 cup strawberries

1 cup blackberries

1 cup granola

1/4 cup tiny marshmallows

Directions

Divide 1/3 of flavored yogurt among four dessert glasses.

Alternate layers of berries and granola with yogurt.

Top with tiny marshmallows and serve immediately.

Pineapple Ice Cream Cake

(Ready in about 30 minutes | Servings 4)

Ingredients

1/2 stick butter

1/4 cup brown sugar, packed

1 tablespoon maple syrup

1/4 teaspoon ground cinnamon

1 cup canned pineapple, drained and chopped

2 cups vanilla ice cream

1 cup pound cake, coarsely crumbled

Whipped cream, as garnish

Directions

In a skillet, melt butter over medium-low heat. Stir in brown sugar, maple syrup, and cinnamon, bringing to a boil. Reduce the heat and then cook for another 2 minutes.

Add pineapple and stir again to combine. Cook for 2 minutes more or until it is heated through. Turn off the heat.

Scoop vanilla ice cream into four dessert bowls. Place crumbled pound cake over the ice cream.

Top with warm pineapple mixture and whipped cream. Serve immediately and enjoy!

Nutty Butterscotch Bars

(Ready in about 2 hours 25 minutes | Servings 16)

Ingredients

Non-stick cooking spray

1 ½ cups powdered sugar

1 cup peanut butter

6 tablespoons coconut oil, melted

2 cups crushed pretzels

2 cups butterscotch-flavored pieces

1/4 cup whipping cream

1/2 cup coarsely crushed pretzels

1/2 cup walnuts, chopped

Directions

Line a square pan with an aluminum foil. Then, coat the foil with non-stick cooking spray and set aside.

In a mixing bowl, stir together powdered sugar, peanut butter, and melted coconut oil. Stir in crushed pretzels. Next, press the mixture into the bottom of prepared baking pan.

In a saucepan, combine butterscotch pieces and whipping cream over low heat, stirring often.

Then, spoon and spread butterscotch mixture over the mixture in the square pan. Sprinkle crushed pretzels and the walnuts evenly over butterscotch mixture in the square pan; press gently and set aside.

Chill for about 2 hours before cutting into bars. You can store these bars in your refrigerator for up to 1 week. Enjoy!

Yummiest Strawberry Banana Trifle

(Ready in about 15 minutes | Servings 6)

Ingredients

1 (4-serving-size) package instant vanilla pudding

3 ripe bananas, sliced

1 teaspoon grated ginger

1 teaspoon fresh lemon juice

1 cup strawberries, sliced

3 packs shortbread cookies, broken

6 maraschino cherries with stems, as garnish

Directions

Start by preparing pudding mix according to manufacturer's directions.

Divide prepared pudding among 6 dessert dishes. Then, layer bananas; sprinkle with grated ginger and drizzle with lemon juice.

Then, layer the strawberries and broken shortbread cookies. Garnish with maraschino cherries and serve!

Banana Coffee Mousse

(Ready in about 15 minutes | Servings 6)

Ingredients

1 ½ cups chocolate milk

2 teaspoons instant coffee crystals

1 (4-serving-size) package instant pudding mix

1 ¼ ounces envelope whipped dessert topping mix

2 cups banana, sliced

Chocolate curls, for garnish

Directions

In a measuring cup or a large-sized mixing bowl, combine chocolate milk and instant coffee crystals. Allow to stand for about 5 minutes.

Stir in instant pudding mix and whipped dessert topping mix. Then, beat with an electric mixer on low speed about 1/2 minute. After that, mix on high speed about 4 minutes more.

Alternately spoon prepared mousse and bananas into 6 water goblets. Serve chilled and garnished with chocolate curls. Enjoy!

Superfast Fruit Cheesecake

(Ready in about 20 minutes | Servings 4)

Ingredients

1/2 cup cream cheese, softened

1/4 cup Brie cheese, softened and without the rind

3 tablespoons sugar

1 teaspoon fresh orange juice

1 cup strawberries, sliced

1 cup pineapple, sliced

1/2 cup slivered almonds

Directions

In a medium-sized mixing bowl, beat the cream cheese, Brie, sugar, and orange juice with an electric mixer on medium speed. Reserve.

Place half of the strawberries and half of the pineapple in four parfait glasses.

Top with half of the cheese mixture. Repeat layers one more time. Scatter the almonds on top and serve.

Blueberry Crumb Bars

(Ready in about 1 hour 5 minutes | Servings 16)

Ingredients

Non-stick cooking spray

1 (17.5-ounce) package oatmeal cookie mix

1/2 cup margarine

1 egg, beaten

1/2 teaspoon anise seed

1 teaspoon almond extract

2 cups blueberries

1/4 cup sugar

Icing sugar, as garnish

Directions

Begin by preheating an oven to 350 degrees F. Coat your baking pan with a foil; lightly coat foil with non-stick cooking spray.

Arrange oatmeal cookie mix in a large-sized bowl. Then, cut in the margarine and mix until mixture resembles coarse crumbs. Reserve 1 cup of the oatmeal mixture for the topping.

Next, add the egg, anise seed and almond extract to the remaining crumb mixture.

Press the mixture evenly onto the bottom of the baking pan.

In another bowl, combine together blueberries and sugar; spread evenly over mixture in the baking pan. Sprinkle with the oatmeal crumb mixture.

Bake about 45 minutes; then, remove to a wire rack. Dust with icing sugar and allow to cool completely.

Cut into bars, transfer to a nice serving platter, and serve.

Tropical Refreshing Wontons

(Ready in about 20 minutes | Servings 4)

Ingredients

Non-stick cooking spray

8 wonton wrappers

3 tablespoons granulated sugar

1/2 cup bananas, sliced

1/4 cup pineapple, broken into chunks

2 kiwi fruit, sliced

3/4 cup lemon yogurt

4 maraschino cherries with stems, for garnish

Directions

Preheat your oven to 350 degrees F. Coat your baking sheet with a foil; lightly grease with non-stick cooking spray.

Arrange wonton wrappers flat on the baking sheet; lightly grease with non-stick cooking spray. Sprinkle with granulated sugar.

Bake your wontons for about 8 minutes or until they're golden brown and crisp. Allow to cool slightly.

In the meantime, combine together the bananas, pineapple, and the kiwi fruit.

Place baked wontons on four dessert plates. Top each wonton with the lemon yogurt, reserving a small amount for the topping. Then, divide the fruit mixture evenly among the stacks.

Place another baked wonton on the top. Top with remaining lemon yogurt. Garnish with maraschino cherries and serve.

Chocolate Cherry Cake

(Ready in about 20 minutes | Servings 16)

Ingredients

1 package chocolate fudge cake mix

2 (10-ounce) jars cherry preserves

2 tablespoons brandy

Whipped cream, as garnish

Chocolate curls, as garnish

Directions

First of all, butter a suitable baking pan. Prepare the cake mix according to manufacturer's directions. Set aside your cake on a wire rack in order to cool.

Next, in a bowl, mix together the cherry preserves and the brandy. Cut prepared cake into squares.

Top with whipped cream and fruit mixture. Sprinkle with chocolate curls. Serve chilled and enjoy!

Aromatic Apple Dessert with Ice Cream

(Ready in about 20 minutes | Servings 4)

Ingredients

2 tablespoons butter

2 apples, cored and sliced

1/4 teaspoon ground ginger

1/4 teaspoon ground cinnamon

1 teaspoon pure vanilla extract

3 tablespoons packed brown sugar

1/3 cup apple juice

1 teaspoon cornstarch

2 cups vanilla ice cream

Directions

Melt the butter in the skillet over medium heat; then, cook the apples with ground ginger until your apples are just tender or about 3 minutes.

Stir in the cinnamon, vanilla extract, and sugar.

In a small-sized mixing bowl, combine together apple juice and cornstarch; add this mixture to the skillet.

Cook until the mixture is thickened. Allow to cool slightly.

Scoop vanilla ice cream into 4 dessert bowls. Top with apple mixture and serve.

Pineapple with Lime Sherbet

(Ready in about 25 minutes | Servings 4)

Ingredients

1 cup canned pineapple chunks with juice

1/3 cup orange marmalade

1/4 teaspoon ground cinnamon

1/4 teaspoon grated nutmeg

1/4 teaspoon ground ginger

1 ¼ cups canned mandarin orange sections, drained

2 cups lime sherbet

Directions

Add all the above ingredients, except the lime sherbet, to a medium bowl. Gently toss to coat.

Set aside in the freezer for 15 minutes, stirring occasionally.

Spoon lime sherbet into 4 chilled dessert bowls. Then, top each with fruit mixture. Serve and enjoy!

Brownie Mint Parfaits

(Ready in about 25 minutes | Servings 4)

Ingredients

1 cup cream cheese, softened

3 tablespoons honey

1 tablespoon whole milk

4 squares milk chocolate brownies, broken into chunks

8 cream-filled mint patties, broken into chunks

Whipped cream (optional)

4 maraschino cherries with stems, for garnish (optional)

Directions

Blend the cheese, honey and whole milk in a food processor or a blender. Process till creamy and smooth.

Then, chill in the refrigerator for 20 minutes.

To serve: Alternately layer cheese mixture, chocolate brownies, and cream-filled mint patties in 4 chilled parfait glasses.

Top with whipped cream and garnish with maraschino cherries, if used. Serve immediately and enjoy!

Easiest and Yummiest Chocolate Panini

(Ready in about 20 minutes | Servings 4)

Ingredients

8 slices challah bread

2 tablespoons butter, melted

3/4 cup chocolate pieces

Powdered sugar

Directions

Heat a large nonstick skillet over medium flame. Then, brush each bread slice with some of the butter.

Place 4 bread slices on a work surface; sprinkle with chocolate pieces. Top with remaining bread slices. Place sandwiches in a hot skillet.

Grill the sandwiches for 6 to 8 minutes; the chocolate should be melted and bread should be golden brown.

Slice each sandwich into quarters and dust them with powdered sugar. You can garnish the sandwiches with your favorite fruit such as banana, apple, strawberry and so on. Serve warm and enjoy.

Cinnamon Puff Cookies

(Ready in about 25 minutes | Servings 6)

Ingredients

1 rolled unbaked pie crust

2 tablespoons butter, melted

1/4 teaspoon ground cinnamon

1/2 teaspoon anise seed

1 teaspoon pure vanilla extract

2 tablespoons packed brown sugar

1 teaspoon pumpkin pie spice

Directions

Begin by preheating an oven to 400 degrees F. Unroll your pie crust according to manufacturer's directions.

Place the crust on a lightly floured surface. Then, brush the pie crust with the butter. Sprinkle with ground cinnamon, anise seed, pure vanilla extract, brown sugar, and pumpkin pie spice.

Use a cookie or pizza cutter to cut dough into small squares. Transfer the squares to a large cookie sheet.

Bake approximately 10 minutes and transfer to a wire rack in order to cool slightly. Dust with powdered sugar if desired. Enjoy!

Spiced Chocolate Mint Bars

(Ready in about 30 minutes + chilling time | Servings 8)

Ingredients

Non-stick cooking spray

1 cup rolled oats

1/2 cup dark chocolate pieces

6 tablespoons butter, softened

A pinch of salt

A pinch of ground cinnamon

A pinch of grated nutmeg

19 chocolate wafers, crushed

1 tablespoon cocoa powder

1 tablespoon whole milk

1/2 teaspoon shortening

3/4 cup powdered sugar

1/4 cup cream cheese, room temperature

1/2 teaspoon pure peppermint extract

Snipped fresh mint, as garnish

Directions

Coat a pan with non-stick cooking spray.

To prepare the crust, place rolled oats in a food processor; pulse with several on/off turns until it' finely ground.

In a saucepan, combine together 1/4 cup of the dark chocolate pieces and the butter; cook over low heat until melted; stir frequently.

Stir in oats, salt, cinnamon, nutmeg, crushed wafers, cocoa powder, and milk. Press this mixture into the greased pan. Allow to cool in your fridge for about 30 minutes.

In the same saucepan, combine the remaining 1/4 cup chocolate pieces with the shortening. Then, cook over low heat until the mixture is combined and melted. Reserve.

Next, add powdered sugar, cream cheese, and peppermint extract to a medium-sized mixing bowl; stir until everything is uniform and smooth.

Spread the mixture evenly over the crust in the pan. Drizzle with the chocolate mixture.

Chill until the chocolate is set or about 1 hour. Cut into 24 bars and garnish with fresh mint. Serve.

Coconut Apple Crumble

(Ready in about 30 minutes | Servings 4)

Ingredients

4 apples, peeled, cored and sliced

1/4 cup golden raisins

1 teaspoon coconut extract

1 teaspoon vanilla extract

3 tablespoons brown sugar

1 teaspoon apple pie spice

3 tablespoons butter, cold

1 ½ cups low-fat granola

1/4 cup coconut, shredded

Whipped cream, as garnish

Directions

Start by preheating an oven to 375 degrees F.

Arrange the apples and golden raisins in a square baking dish. Stir in coconut extract and vanilla extract.

Next, sprinkle with brown sugar and apple pie spice. Cut in the butter. Scatter the granola and shredded coconut evenly over apple mixture.

Bake 13 to 15 minutes or till the apples are heated through.

Divide among four dessert dishes, top with whipped cream and serve warm.

Ice Cream Surprise

(Ready in about 20 minutes | Servings 4)

Ingredients

1/2 cup hot ice cream topping

1 tablespoon coffee liqueur

2 cups vanilla ice cream

4 waffle cones

1/4 cup raspberries

1/4 cup strawberries, sliced

Chocolate syrup, as garnish

Directions

In a saucepan, cook ice cream topping and coffee liqueur over medium-low heat. Remove saucepan from the heat and set aside.

Then, scoop ice cream into waffle cones.

Top with raspberries and strawberries. Drizzle with chocolate syrup and serve!

Berry Frozen Yogurt Dessert

(Ready in about 15 minutes | Servings 6)

Ingredients

4 cups vanilla frozen yogurt

1 ½ cups fresh mixed berries

1 cup toasted coconut

3 tablespoons honey

Fresh mint leaves, as garnish

Directions

Divide yogurt among six water goblets.

Top each serving with mixed berries and toasted coconut.

Drizzle with honey and garnish with fresh mint leaves. Enjoy!

Fruit and Almond Ice Cream Dessert

(Ready in about 15 minutes | Servings 6)

Ingredients

4 cups vanilla ice cream

1 cup pineapple chunks

1/2 cup banana, sliced

1 cup toasted almonds, slivered

3 tablespoons honey

Chocolate shavings, as garnish

Directions

Divide the ice cream among 6 dessert dishes.

Top each serving with pineapple chunks, banana, and slivered almonds.

Drizzle with honey; garnish with chocolate shavings. Serve.

Nutty Coffee Banana Dessert

(Ready in about 25 minutes | Servings 4)

Ingredients

1/4 cup sugar

3 tablespoons coffee-flavored liqueur

3 tablespoons butter

3 bananas, sliced

1/2 teaspoon grated nutmeg

1/4 teaspoon ground cloves

1/2 teaspoon ground cinnamon

2 cups vanilla frozen yogurt

Slivered and toasted almonds, as garnish

Directions

Begin by preheating an oven to 400 degrees F.

Sprinkle the bottom of a casserole dish with sugar. Pour coffee-flavored liqueur. Cut in the butter.

Add banana slices; sprinkle with nutmeg, cloves, and cinnamon. Bake about 15 minutes.

Divide vanilla frozen yogurt among 4 dessert bowls. Spoon baked mixture over frozen yogurt. Scatter the slivered almonds over the top and serve.

Melt in Your Mouth Nutty Bars

(Ready in about 30 minutes | Servings 16)

Ingredients

Non-stick cooking spray

1 cup packed brown sugar

1/2 cup peanut butter

1/4 cup canola oil

1/2 teaspoon allspice

1/2 teaspoon ground cinnamon

1/4 teaspoon salt

2 eggs, lightly beaten

1/4 cup milk

1 1/2 cups self-rising flour

3/4 cup peanut butter-flavored pieces

1/2 cup walnuts coarsely chopped

Directions

Start by preheating an oven to 350 degrees F. Lightly coat s baking pan with non-stick cooking spray; set aside.

In a mixing bowl, beat together the brown sugar, peanut butter, canola oil, allspice, ground cinnamon, salt, and eggs; mix until everything is well blended.

Pour in the milk; mix to combine; add the flour and mix again. Spread the mixture into a prepared pan.

Sprinkle peanut butter-flavored pieces and walnuts on the top. Bake approximately 20 minutes or until a wooden stick inserted in center comes out clean.

Transfer to a wire rack. Cut into 32 bars and transfer to a serving platter. Serve and enjoy!

Cheesy Banana Cake

(Ready in about 1 hour 15 minutes | Servings 16)

Ingredients

3 ripe bananas, mashed

2 teaspoons orange juice

3 cups all-purpose flour

1 teaspoon baking soda

1/2 teaspoon baking powder

A pinch of salt

3/4 cup butter, softened

2 cups sugar

3 large-sized eggs

1 teaspoon pure vanilla extract

1 ½ cups buttermilk

For the Frosting:

1/2 cup butter, softened

1 cup cream cheese, softened

1 teaspoon pure almond extract

3 ½ cups powdered sugar

For the Garnish:

Almonds, coarsely chopped

Directions

Preheat your oven to 275 degrees F. Butter and flour your baking pan.

In a bowl, mix mashed banana with the orange juice; reserve. In a separate medium-sized bowl, mix flour, baking soda, baking powder, and salt; reserve.

In another mixing bowl, cream the butter with sugar until the mixture becomes fluffy. Stir in the eggs, vanilla, and buttermilk. Stir in the flour mixture and banana mixture.

Next, pour the batter into prepared baking pan; bake for one hour or until a toothpick inserted in center comes out clean. Place into the freezer for 45 minutes.

To prepare the frosting, cream the butter and cream cheese until the mixture is well combined and smooth. Add the almond extract and powdered sugar and beat until your mixture is well combined.

Spread the frosting onto the cooled cake. Sprinkle with chopped almonds and serve!

Tea Party Chewy Cookies

(Ready in about 20 minutes | Servings 16)

Ingredients

1 (18.25-ounce) box dry cake mix

1/2 cup coconut oil

2 large-sized eggs

1/4 teaspoon ground cinnamon

1/2 teaspoon anise seed

Confectioners' sugar, for rolling

Directions

Begin by preheating an oven to 350 degrees F.

Stir dry cake mix, coconut oil, eggs, ground cinnamon and anise seed in a large-sized mixing bowl.

Then, dust your hands with confectioners' sugar and shape your dough into bite-sized balls.

Roll balls in confectioners' sugar and transfer them to the cookie sheets.

Bake for about 10 minutes. Allow to cool on wire racks and serve.

Peach Dump Cake

(Ready in about 3 hours 5 minutes | Servings 8)

Ingredients

2 cups peaches, pitted and sliced

1 tablespoon cornstarch

1/4 teaspoon anise seed

1/4 teaspoon ground cinnamon

1/2 teaspoon pure vanilla extract

1/4 cup brown sugar

4 tablespoons margarine or butter, melted

1/2 package of a 2-layer size cake mix

Directions

Treat the inside of your slow cooker with vegetable shortening; arrange the peach slices in the bottom. Sprinkle with cornstarch; toss to combine.

Sprinkle anise seed, cinnamon, vanilla, and brown sugar over all.

Drizzle melted margarine or butter evenly over cake mix. Cover and cook on high for about 3 hours. Serve at room temperature with a dollop of whipped cream, if desired.

Apricot and Peach Cobbler

(Ready in about 1 hour | Servings 6)

Ingredients

4 large-sized fresh apricots, pitted and quartered

2 large-sized fresh peaches, pitted, peeled and sliced

1 cup granulated sugar

1/2 cup butter, melted

1 cup flour

1/2 cup brown sugar

1 teaspoon baking soda

1 teaspoon baking powder

1/4 teaspoon salt

1 dash of cinnamon

1 dash of allspice

3/4 cup whole milk

Directions

Begin by preheating an oven to 375 degrees F.

Mix apricot and peach slices with 1 cup of granulated sugar; set aside.

Add the butter to a square baking dish.

In another mixing bowl, mix together the rest of the above ingredients. Mix to combine well. Pour over butter in the baking dish.

Top with tossed apricots and peaches. Bake for 45 minutes and serve warm.

Aromatic Peach Cobbler with Almonds

(Ready in about 50 minutes | Servings 8)

Ingredients

6 ripe peaches, peeled, pitted and sliced

2/3 cup sugar

1 teaspoon grated lemon rind

1 teaspoon grated orange rind

1 tablespoon orange juice

1/2 teaspoon vanilla extract

1/2 teaspoon almond extract

1 ½ cups flour

1 tablespoon baking powder

1/3 cup vegetable shortening

1 large-sized egg, lightly beaten

1/4 cup fat-free milk

1 teaspoon cardamom

2 tablespoons cinnamon sugar

For the Topping:

1 cup heavy cream

2 tablespoons brandy

For the garnish:

Slivered almonds, toasted

Directions

Preheat your oven to 400 degrees F. Lightly grease a baking dish with vegetable shortening.

In a mixing bowl, toss the peaches with 2/3 cup of sugar.

In another mixing bowl, place lemon rind, orange rind, orange juice, vanilla, almond extract, flour, and baking powder; thoroughly stir until everything is well combined.

In a separate bowl, mix together the vegetable shortening, egg, milk, and cardamom. Mix to combine well. Add this wet mixture to the dry mixture. Mix to combine well.

Pour the batter into your baking dish. Top with tossed peaches. Sprinkle with cinnamon sugar.

Bake for about 20 minutes.

To prepare the topping: Whip heavy cream to soft peaks; flavor with 2 tablespoons brandy.

Serve your peach cobbler warm, garnished with slivered toasted almonds, accompanied by prepared topping. Enjoy!

Gooey Chocolate Cherry Pie

(Ready in about 1 hour | Servings 16)

Ingredients

2 (20-ounce) cans cherry pie filling

1 (18.5-ounce) box chocolate cake mix, unprepared

1/2 teaspoon cardamom

1 teaspoon orange juice

3⁄4 cup butter, melted

Directions

Start by preheating your oven to 350 degrees F. Then, dump pie filling into a cake pan.

Spread chocolate cake mix evenly over pie filling in the cake pan. Sprinkle with cardamom and drizzle with orange juice.

Drizzle melted butter over all.

Bake for 1 hour. Serve at room temperature or chilled if you like.

Slow Cooker Nut Candy

(Ready in about 2 hours | Servings 24)

Ingredients

1 cup walnuts, halved

2 cup dry roasted almonds

2 cups dry roasted peanuts

1 (12-ounce) package chocolate chips

4 ounces chocolate bars

32 ounces white almond bark

Directions

Put walnuts, almonds and peanuts into the bottom of your slow cooker (crock pot); add other ingredients.

Slow cook on low setting for 2 hours.

Then, drop rounded spoonfuls onto wax paper; allow to cool completely before serving.

Transfer to a serving platter and enjoy!

Chocolate Mud Cake with Ice Cream

(Ready in about 2 hours 30 minutes | Servings 6)

Ingredients

1 cup all-purpose flour

1 teaspoon baking soda

1 teaspoon baking powder

6 tablespoons butter

1/4 cup chocolate chips

1 cup sugar

A dash of cardamom

A dash of cinnamon

1 teaspoon pure almond extract

1 tablespoon pure vanilla extract

A pinch of salt

1/3 cup milk

1 egg yolk

1/3 cup cocoa powder

1 ½ cups hot water

Ice cream, as garnish

Directions

Coat the inside of a slow cooker with non-stick cooking spray or vegetable shortening.

Sift together the flour, baking soda and baking powder in a medium-sized bowl. In a microwavable bowl, place the butter and chocolate chips; melt them in the microwave.

Whisk together the 2/3 cup of sugar, cardamom, cinnamon, almond, vanilla, salt, milk, and egg yolk. Add the flour mixture; mix until everything is well combined.

Pour the batter into the greased slow cooker.

In a medium bowl, whisk together the remaining sugar, cocoa powder and hot water until the sugar is dissolved. Pour this mixture over the batter in the slow cooker.

Cook 2 ¼ hours on high. Allow to cool for about 30 minutes. Then, divide among 6 dessert bowls and top with your favorite ice cream. Serve.

Crock Pot Pumpkin Pie

(Ready in about 7 hours | Servings 6)

Ingredients

1 (15-ounce) can pumpkin

1 ¼ cups milk

3⁄4 cup granulated sugar

1⁄2 cup Bisquick mix

2 eggs, beaten

2 tablespoons butter, melted

2 teaspoons pumpkin pie spice

1 teaspoon vanilla extract

Whipped topping, as garnish

Directions

Treat your crock pot (slow cooker) with non-stick cooking spray.

In a large-sized mixing bowl, combine together all the above ingredient, except whipped topping.

Transfer the mixture to the prepared crock pot. Cover with the lid; cook on low about 7 hours.

Serve in 6 dessert bowls with whipped cream. Enjoy!

Overnight Pear and Apple Dessert

(Ready in about 9 hours | Servings 2)

Ingredients

2 pears, peeled and sliced

2 medium-sized apples, peeled and sliced

1⁄4 cup maple syrup

1/4 teaspoon ground cloves

1/4 teaspoon grated nutmeg

1 teaspoon cinnamon

2 tablespoons butter, melted

2 cups granola cereal

Directions

Place pears and apples in a slow cooker; add the rest of the above ingredients.

Cover with the lid and slow cook on low 8 to 9 hours or overnight.

Serve with a dollop of whipped cream or vanilla ice cream, if desired.

Slow Cooker Cherry Cobbler

(Ready in about 1 hour 40 minutes | Servings 6)

Ingredients

1 (21-ounce) can cherry pie filling

1 cup all-purpose flour

1/4 cup brown sugar

1/4 cup margarine, melted

1/2 cup milk, low-fat is fine

1 teaspoons baking powder

1/2 teaspoon vanilla extract

1/2 teaspoon coconut extract

1 cup flaked coconut, toasted

Directions

Lightly grease the sides and bottom of your slow cooker or crock pot with cooking spray or the other vegetable shortening.

Spread the canned cherry pie filling evenly into your slow cooker.

Combine together the remaining ingredients until you get a smooth batter. Spread the batter over the cherry pie filling in the slow cooker.

Cover and cook on high for about 2 hours, or until a skewer pierced into the center of your cobbler comes out clean. Serve at room temperature, accompanied by whipped topping.

Gorgeous Blueberry Dump Cake

(Ready in about 3 hours | Servings 4)

Ingredients

Non-stick cooking spray

1 (21-ounce) can blueberry pie filling

1 (18.25-ounce) package dry white cake mix

1 teaspoon cardamom

1 teaspoon anise seed

1/2 teaspoon almond extract

1/2 cup butter, softened

1/2 cup almonds, toasted and chopped

Directions

Treat the inside of your slow cooker (crock pot) with non-stick cooking spray.

Spread pie filling evenly at the bottom of greased slow cooker.

In a mixing bowl, combine white cake mix, cardamom, anise seed, almond extract, and butter. Sprinkle with almonds; cover and cook on low setting for about 3 hours.

Divide among four nice serving bowls. Top with some extra almonds and vanilla ice cream if desired. Serve!

Vegan Chocolate Cake

(Ready in about 2 hours 35 minutes | Servings 6)

Ingredients

Non-stick cooking spray

1 cup flour

1/2 cup brown sugar

2 tablespoons cocoa powder

1 teaspoon baking soda

1 teaspoon baking powder

A pinch of salt

1/2 cup almond milk

2 tablespoons canola oil

1 teaspoon vanilla extract

1/4 cup cocoa

1 ½ cups hot water

Directions

Grease the inside of your crock pot with non-stick cooking spray.

In a mixing bowl, combine together flour, brown sugar, 2 tablespoons cocoa powder, baking soda, baking powder, and salt.

Pour in the almond milk, canola oil, and pure vanilla extract; mix until smooth. Pour the batter into greased crock pot.

Sprinkle 1/4 cup cocoa over batter in the crock pot. Pour hot water into the crock pot; do not stir.

Slow cook on high for 2 hours or until a wooden stick inserted in center comes out clean. Uncover; let stand for 30 minutes.

Spoon cake into 6 dessert bowls.

Buttered Rum Cream

(Ready in about 5 hours | Servings 8)

Ingredients

2 cups packed brown sugar

1/2 cup butter, softened

1/4 teaspoon salt

1 vanilla bean

2 cinnamon sticks

2 cardamom pods

1/2 teaspoon ground nutmeg

2 cups dark rum

Whipped cream, as garnish

Directions

Put brown sugar, butter, salt, vanilla bean, cinnamon sticks, cardamom pods, nutmeg, dark rum into your crock pot.

Add 8 cups of hot water; stir well to combine. Cook on low heat setting for 5 hours.

Serve in warm mugs with a scoop of whipped cream. Enjoy!

Superfine Caramel Pie

(Ready in about 7 hours | Servings 8)

Ingredients

2 (14-ounce) cans sweetened milk

1 graham cracker crust

1 cup whipped topping

1 English candy bar, coarsely chopped

Directions

Pour condensed milk into your slow cooker.

Cover with the lid; cook approximately 7 hours, stirring your mixture every 30 minutes. Pour prepared mixture into graham cracker crust; allow to cool completely.

Spread whipped topping over top; top with chopped candy bar. Serve chilled and enjoy!

Almond Butter Cookies

(Ready in about 35 minutes | Servings 10)

Ingredients

Vegetable shortening or non-stick cooking spray

2 cups peanut butter

2 cups sugar

2 large-sized eggs, beaten

1/2 teaspoon grated ginger

2 teaspoons baking powder

1/4 teaspoon cardamom

1/2 teaspoon grated nutmeg

1/2 teaspoon ground cinnamon

1 teaspoon pure almond extract

Directions

Begin by preheating an oven to 350 degrees F. Lightly grease your cookie sheets with vegetable shortening or non-stick cooking spray.

In a medium-sized mixing bowl, combine together peanut butter and sugar. Add the eggs; stir in the ginger, baking powder, cardamom, nutmeg, cinnamon, and pure almond extract.

Mix until your dough is smooth and elastic. Shape the dough into bite-sized balls; place the balls onto the greased cookie sheets. Press the cookies with the back of a fork.

Bake approximately 12 minutes. Transfer to a cooling rack. Allow to cool completely before serving. Enjoy!

Twirly Lemon Cookies

(Ready in about 35 minutes | Servings 15)

Ingredients

2 sticks unsalted butter, softened

1/3 cup sugar

3/4 cup powdered sugar

1 teaspoon anise seed

1/2 teaspoon cardamom

4 large egg yolks

1 tablespoon lemon zest

2 tablespoons fresh lemon juice

1 teaspoon vanilla extract

1/2 teaspoon lemon extract

2 ¼ cups flour

1/2 teaspoon baking powder

1/2 teaspoon baking soda

1/8 teaspoon salt

Directions

Preheat an oven to 350 degrees F. Coat a cookie sheet with a foil and lightly spray with cooking spray.

Then, whiz the butter with sugar and powdered sugar in a food processor until everything is well mixed. Add the anise seed, cardamom, egg yolks, lemon zest, lemon juice, vanilla and lemon extract; then, whiz until everything is thoroughly mixed.

Add the flour, baking powder, baking soda and salt, and mix again to combine well.

Transfer the dough to a pastry bag fitted with open star tip and pipe circular swirls onto the baking sheet.

Bake your cookies about 10 minutes, or until the cookies are just golden brown.

Transfer the cookies to a cooling rack; allow to cool completely before serving.

Homemade Chocolate Eclair

(Ready in about 20 minutes | Servings 12)

Ingredients

2 small packages instant vanilla pudding mix

3 cups whole milk

1 cup whipped topping

1 (16-ounce) box graham crackers

1 (15-ounce) container chocolate frosting

Directions

In a bowl or a measuring cup, combine together vanilla pudding and whole milk. Then, fold in whipped topping.

Line a square pan with one layer of graham crackers. Place 1/2 of the pudding mixture over the graham crackers.

Place the other layer of graham crackers. Place the remaining pudding mixture over the graham crackers.

Then, place a third layer of graham crackers.

Melt the chocolate frosting in the microwave for 30 seconds. Spread frosting on the top of your cake.

Cover and allow to set for 3 hours in the refrigerator. Cut into squares and serve.

Greek Yogurt with Fruits

(Ready in about 15 minutes | Servings 4)

Ingredients

1 (8-ounce) plain Greek yogurt

4 tablespoons honey

1 cup blueberries, roughly chopped

1/2 cup bananas, sliced

Almonds, chopped and toasted

Directions

Divide Greek yogurt among four ice cream bowls.

Then, add honey. Top with blueberries and bananas. Sprinkle with chopped almonds and serve.

Peanut Butter and Yogurt Delight

(Ready in about 2 hours 15 minutes | Servings 16)

Ingredients

8 cups vanilla flavored yogurt, frozen

1 (1.5-ounce) box instant chocolate pudding mix

1/2 cup peanut butter

1 cup whipped topping

Chocolate fudge topping, as garnish

Directions

In a large-sized mixing bowl, combine the frozen yogurt, pudding mix, and peanut butter. Fold in whipped topping.

Spoon the mixture into a pan. Drizzle with chocolate fudge topping. Freeze at least 2 hours.

Slice into 16 pieces and serve immediately.

Lazy Woman's Baklava

(Ready in about 50 minutes | Servings 20)

Ingredients

1 box phyllo dough, thawed

1 cup margarine, melted

For the Syrup:

1 cup sugar

1/2 cup water

1/2 teaspoon ground cloves

1/2 teaspoon cardamom

1 teaspoon pure vanilla extract

1 teaspoon lemon juice

For the Filling:

1/2 cup walnuts, finely chopped

1/2 cup almonds, finely chopped

1/2 cup sugar

1 teaspoon ground cinnamon

Directions

Place 1 cup sugar, water, cloves, cardamom, vanilla extract and lemon juice in a saucepan; bring to a boil over medium heat.

Then, reduce the heat to medium-low and simmer the syrup for 5 minutes, stirring occasionally; allow to cool.

Lay out phyllo dough; trim to fit your square baking pan. Cut the dough in half; place 1/2 of dough in the baking pan.

In a mixing bowl, combine together the filling ingredients; spread prepared filling over phyllo dough.

Top with the second half of phyllo dough. Cut your baklava into triangles with a sharp knife. Drizzle evenly with melted margarine.

Bake at 350 degrees for 30 minutes, till the top is golden brown. Afterwards, pour cooled syrup over hot baklava and serve.

Low-Fat Peanut Butter Mousse

(Ready in about 1 hour 10 minutes | Servings 6)

Ingredients

2 tablespoons water

2 tablespoons peanut butter

1 cup cool whip

2 cups milk

1 (3 1/4 ounce) package vegetarian instant pudding mix

Chocolate curls, as garnish

Directions

Combine 2 tablespoons of water with the peanut butter. Then, add the cool whip and mix to combine well.

Pour 2 cups milk into a mixing bowl or a measuring cup. Add the pudding mix; whisk until everything is well combined.

Add the peanut butter mixture to the pudding mixture. Chill for about 1 hour.

Divide among 6 dessert glasses, sprinkle with chocolate curls and enjoy!

Rich Dessert Salad

(Ready in about 2 hours 5 minutes | Servings 12)

Ingredients

12 ounces whipped cream

1 cup flavored milk

1 (15-ounce) can cherry pie filling or

1 (15-ounce) can crushed pineapple

1 cup flaked coconut

Directions

In a large-sized bowl, mix together the whipped cream and flavored milk. Mix to combine well.

Add the rest of the above ingredients.

Set in a refrigerator for about 2 hours before serving; sprinkle with some extra nuts if desired and enjoy.

Cottage and Peach Dessert

(Ready in about 15 minutes + chilling time | Servings 6)

Ingredients

2 cups cottage cheese

1 (1/3-ounce) dry strawberry gelatin

1/2 cup cool whip

2 cups peaches, pitted, peeled and sliced

Directions

In a blender or a food processor, pulse the cottage cheese until creamy and smooth. Transfer to a dessert bowl.

Sprinkle with gelatin over top; add cool whip and peaches. Gently stir to combine well.

Refrigerate about 3 hours before serving. Indulge your sweet tooth with this easy and delicious dessert!

Delicious Lime Pie

(Ready in about 15 minutes + chilling time | Servings 8)

Ingredients

1 (14-ounce) can condensed milk

1/2 teaspoon cardamom

1/2 teaspoon grated ginger

1/2 cup lime juice

1 cup whipped topping

1 (6-ounce) package graham cracker pie crusts

Directions

Beat milk, cardamom, ginger and lime juice with an electric mixer on medium speed; beat until the mixture is smooth and thickened.

Fold in whipped topping.

Spoon this mixture into graham cracker pie crust. Cover and refrigerate about 1 hour. Serve.

White Chocolate Butter Cake

(Ready in about 35 minutes | Servings 12)

Ingredients

For the Brownie:

1 ½ cups butter

1 ½ cups sugar

1 ½ cups flour

1 teaspoon baking powder

1/4 teaspoon salt

2 eggs, lightly beaten

1 teaspoon vanilla

1 cup pecans

1 cup white chocolate chips

For the Sauce:

1 1/3 cups sugar

1 cup whipping cream

2/3 cup butter

Directions

Begin by preheating an oven to 350 degrees F. Lightly grease a baking pan and set aside.

Blend butter and sugar with an electric mixer. Then, add flour, baking powder, salt, lightly beaten eggs, and vanilla. Mix until everything is well blended and incorporated.

Next, fold in pecans and white chocolate chips. Pour the mixture into the baking pan.

Bake the brownie for about 25 minutes.

Meanwhile, prepare the sauce. Combine all the sauce ingredients in a medium-sized saucepan, bringing the mixture to a boil. Cook for 3 minutes or until the sauce is thickened.

To assemble: Cut warm brownies into 12 squares. Then, drizzle your brownies with sauce and serve.

The Ultimate Almond and Chocolate Dessert

(Ready in about 1 hour 15 minutes | Servings 8)

Ingredients

1 cup flour

3⁄4 cup almonds, chopped

1⁄2 cup butter

1 cup cream cheese, softened

1 cup cool whip, softened

1 cup powdered sugar

2 (3.5-ounce) packages instant chocolate pudding mix

3 cups milk

2 cups cool whip

Directions

Begin by preheating your oven to 325 degrees F.

Mix together the flour, almonds, and butter. Transfer to a baking sheet. Bake for 15 minutes; allow to cool on a wire rack.

Next, mix together cream cheese, cool whip, and powdered sugar. Spread this layer onto cooled first layer.

Next, combine the chocolate pudding mix with 3 cups milk; mix thoroughly to blend well. Spread this layer onto the second layer.

Top with cool whip just before serving.

Fantastic Peanut Butter Bars

(Ready in about 15 minutes | Servings 12)

Ingredients

1 ½ cups graham cracker crumbs

3 ½ cups confectioners' sugar

1 cup butter, melted

1 ½ cups peanut butter

1 ½ cups chocolate chips

Directions

In a mixing bowl, combine together the graham crumbs, sugar, butter, and peanut butter. Blend until everything is well combined.

Next, press your mixture evenly into a pan lined with a sheet of baking paper.

Microwave the chocolate chips until it is melted. Spread over mixture in the pan.

Place in a refrigerator until just set; cut into bars and transfer to a serving platter. Serve.

Flourless Hazelnut Butter Cookies

(Ready in about 20 minutes | Servings 12)

Ingredients

1 cup hazelnut butter

1/2 cup sugar

1/2 cup powdered sugar

1/2 teaspoon ground cloves

1 large-sized egg, beaten

1/2 teaspoon vanilla extract

1/2 teaspoon pure hazelnut extract

1 teaspoon baking soda

1/2 teaspoon baking powder

Directions

Preheat an oven to 350 degrees F. Lightly grease your cookie sheets with vegetable shortening.

Beat together hazelnut butter, sugar, and powdered sugar with an electric mixer until creamy and smooth.

Add cloves, egg, vanilla, hazelnut extract, baking soda, and baking powder. Beat until everything is well combined.

Shape the dough into the balls; replace them on prepared cookie sheets. Flatten the cookies with a fork, making a cross pattern. Bake 10 to 12 minutes or till a golden pale.

Transfer to a wire rack to cool completely. May be kept at room temperature for 5 days.

Hurry Up Mug Cake

(Ready in about 10 minutes | Servings 1)

Ingredients

1 egg, beaten

2 tablespoons butter, softened

2 tablespoons almond flour

1/2 teaspoon Stevia

1/2 teaspoon baking powder

2 tablespoons almond flour

1/4 teaspoon grated ginger

1/2 teaspoon cardamom

1/2 teaspoon ground cinnamon

1/4 teaspoon vanilla extract

Directions

Mix all the above ingredients together in a mug. Then, microwave for 70 seconds on high.

Turn cup upside down into a plate.

Garnish with whipped topping or sprinkle with chopped almonds, if desired. Enjoy!

Chocolate Mug Cake

(Ready in about 10 minutes | Servings 2)

Ingredients

4 tablespoons self-rising flour

4 tablespoons white sugar

1 egg

4 tablespoons cocoa powder

5 tablespoons milk

3 tablespoons canola oil

Directions

Combine all the above ingredients together in a large coffee mug. Whisk well until creamy and smooth.

Microwave on high for 3 minutes.

Top with whipping topping and chocolate syrup if desired. Serve.

Superfast Nutty Chocolate Dessert

(Ready in about 10 minutes | Servings 1)

Ingredients

1/8 cup nut butter

2 tablespoons honey

1 tablespoon cocoa powder

1 ½ tablespoons oat flour

1 teaspoon flaked coconut

1/2 teaspoon baking powder

1 large-sized egg, beaten

1 ½ tablespoons chocolate chips

1/2 teaspoon vanilla extract

1/8 teaspoon salt

Directions

Melt the nut butter in a mug for 35 seconds.

Then, add remaining ingredients and stir until everything is well blended and incorporated.

Microwave for 1 minute 30 seconds. Enjoy!

Refreshing Lemon Mug Cake

(Ready in about 10 minutes | Servings 1)

Ingredients

Non-stick cooking spray

3 tablespoons flour

1/2 teaspoon baking powder

1/2 teaspoon ground mace

1/2 teaspoon grated nutmeg

1/4 teaspoon grated ginger root

3 tablespoons granulated sugar

1 whole egg

2 tablespoons canola oil

1 teaspoon lemon rind

1 tablespoon fresh lemon juice

1 tablespoon icing sugar

Directions

Grease your mug with non-stick cooking spray.

In a bowl, mix together flour, baking powder, mace, nutmeg, ginger, and granulated sugar. Mix until everything is well incorporated.

Beat in the egg, oil, lemon rind and lemon juice; beat vigorously until everything is well blended.

Pour into greased mug; microwave for 1 minute 30 seconds on High. Dust with icing sugar and serve.

Mother's Day Mug Cake

(Ready in about 10 minutes | Servings 1)

Ingredients

1/3 cup flour

1/4 cup sugar

1/4 teaspoon baking soda

1/4 teaspoon baking powder

1/2 teaspoon anise seed

1/4 teaspoon cinnamon

A pinch of salt

1 small-sized banana, mashed

1 tablespoon butter, melted

2 tablespoons applesauce

1 large egg yolk

1/2 teaspoon vanilla extract

2 tablespoons walnuts, chopped

Directions

In a large-sized mixing bowl, place all the above ingredients, except the walnuts. Mix to combine well. Transfer to the mug.

Cook your batter in the microwave on high power for about 3 minutes.

Enjoy warm with ice cream if desired!

Mint Vanilla Ice Cream

(Ready in about 20 minutes + chilling time| Servings 10)

Ingredients

1 cup chilled milk

3⁄4 cup white sugar

1/2 teaspoon grated ginger root

2 cups chilled heavy cream

1/2 teaspoon pure mint extract

1 teaspoon pure vanilla extract

2⁄3 cup cake mix

Fresh mint leaves, as garnish

Directions

In a medium-sized mixing bowl, place the milk and sugar; mix until the sugar is completely dissolved.

Stir in the ginger, heavy cream, mint extract, and vanilla. Stir in cake mix; mix to combine.

Pour the mixture into the freezer bowl and allow to stand for about 30 minutes. Then transfer your ice cream to a container.

Divide among 10 ice cream bowls, garnish with fresh mint leaves, serve and enjoy.

Buttermilk Cherry Ice Cream

(Ready in about 5 hours | Servings 6)

Ingredients

2 cups half-and-half

1 cup buttermilk

1 cup heavy cream

1 teaspoon vanilla extract

6 egg yolks

1 1/3 cups white sugar

3 tablespoons sugar, divided

2 cups cherries, pitted

1 tablespoon corn syrup

2 teaspoons applesauce

Directions

Combine together first 6 ingredients in a medium-sized deep saucepan, over medium-low flame. Cook about 12 minutes, whisking often. Bring to a boil, then, remove the saucepan from the flame.

Fill a large-sized metal bowl halfway with ice water.

Pour the mixture into a metal bowl. Place this bowl in ice water for about 30 minutes. Then, chill your mixture for about 2 hours.

In the meantime, combine together 3 tablespoons of sugar, cherries, corn syrup, and applesauce in another small-sized saucepan; let cook over medium heat, 12 minutes or until the cherries are soft.

Remove from the heat and allow to stand for about 15 minutes. Stir in applesauce. Next, chill cherry mixture at least 2 hours.

Freeze the ice cream mixture for 1 hour; freeze cherry mixture for about 30 minutes. Dollop frozen cherry mixture over ice cream; serve.

Berry Coconut Ice Cream

(Ready in about 6 hours 45 minutes | Servings 6)

Ingredients

1 cup raspberries, chopped

1 cup blueberries, chopped

2 tablespoons granulated white sugar

2 tablespoons water

2 cups evaporated milk

2 cups whole milk

2 tablespoons sugar

1/2 teaspoon ground cardamom

1/2 teaspoon coconut extract

1 teaspoon vanilla extract

A pinch of salt

Directions

In a saucepan, bring raspberries, blueberries, 2 tablespoons of granulated sugar, and water to a boil; turn the heat to low, and simmer 10 minutes more, stirring frequently. Then, allow to cool for about 30 minutes.

Transfer to a container, cover and chill about 3 hours.

Whisk together the rest of the ingredients. Freeze this mixture according to manufacturer's instructions.

Next, remove container with ice cream from ice-cream maker and freeze it for 30 minutes; afterwards, swirl in chilled berry mixture. Freeze your ice cream until firm or for 3 to 4 hours.

Divide among six ice cream bowls; sprinkle with some extra berries or flaked coconut if desired; serve and enjoy!

Walnut Bourbon Ice Cream

(Ready in about 6 hours | Servings 6)

Ingredients

1 (14-ounce) can sweetened condensed milk

1 (5-ounce) can evaporated milk

2 cups whole milk

2 tablespoons sugar

1 teaspoon vanilla extract

1 teaspoon almond extract

1 cup walnuts, coarsely chopped

1/2 tablespoon butter

2 tablespoons bourbon

Directions

Whisk together condensed milk, evaporated milk, whole milk, sugar, vanilla extract, and almond extract; chill for 2 hours.

Pour this milk mixture into freezer container of an ice-cream maker; freeze according to manufacturer's directions.

Remove freezer container from ice-cream maker; then, freeze for about 30 minutes.

Next, cook walnuts and butter in a skillet over medium flame, stirring often, about 8 minutes. Spread butter walnuts on a sheet of wax paper and allow to cool completely.

Add cooled pecans to the ice-cream mixture; stir in bourbon; mix to combine. Freeze the ice-cream mixture approximately 4 hours or until firm.

Serve sprinkled with some extra chopped walnuts, if desired. Enjoy!

Birthday Party Marshmallow Pops

(Ready in about 40 minutes | Servings 20)

Ingredients

1 (16-ounce) package graham crackers, crushed

1/2 teaspoon ground cardamom

2 cups chocolate pieces

20 big marshmallows

Directions

In a shallow bowl, place crushed graham crackers and ground cardamom. Mix to combine.

Next, place the chocolate pieces in the microwave until they are completely melted.

Stick a pick in a marshmallow; dip them in the melted chocolate. Then, dip them in graham crackers mixture.

Transfer to a wax paper to dry before serving.

Yellow Apple Cake

(Ready in about 40 minutes | Servings 6)

Ingredients

1 dry yellow cake mix

2 eggs, lightly beaten

1 (21-ounce) can apple pie filling

1/2 teaspoon ground cinnamon

1/2 teaspoon grated nutmeg

1/2 teaspoon ground mace

Directions

Begin by preheating an oven to 350 degrees F.

Place the dry yellow cake mix in a bowl. Then, add the eggs, apple pie filling, and the spices.

Beat with an electric mixer for about 2 minutes. Pour prepared batter into a lightly greased baking pan.

Bake approximately 35 minutes or until a stick comes out clean.

Chocolate White Wine Cupcakes

(Ready in about 40 minutes | Servings 18)

Ingredients

1 ½ cups all-purpose flour

1 cup sugar

1 teaspoon baking soda

1 teaspoon baking powder

1/2 teaspoon ground cardamom

1 teaspoon cinnamon

1/2 cup cocoa powder

1/2 cup coconut oil

1 teaspoon pure vanilla extract

2 eggs

3/4 cup white wine

1/2 cup dried prunes, pitted and chopped

1/4 cup raisins

2 cups whipped cream, for garnish

Directions

Preheat your oven to 350 degrees F. Prepare paper baking cups.

Into the bowl of an electric mixer, put together the flour, sugar, baking soda, baking powder, cardamom, ground cinnamon, and cocoa.

Add coconut oil, vanilla extract, eggs, and white wine.

Beat at LOW speed for 30 seconds. Then, turn the mixer speed to high and beat an additional 3 minutes.

Stir in the prunes and raisins. Pour the batter into the muffin pan; bake for 20 minutes, till a stick pierced in the center comes out clean.

Transfer to a cooling rack for 15 minutes before slicing and serving. Dollop spoonfuls of whipped cream and serve.

Super Bowl Brownie Cookies

(Ready in about 30 minutes | Servings 12)

Ingredients

1 (23 2/3 ounces) package brownie mix

2 eggs

1/2 teaspoon ground cardamom

1/2 teaspoon anise seed

1/2 teaspoon ground mace

1/3 cup coconut oil

3/4 cup chocolate morsels

1/2 cup walnuts, chopped

Directions

Begin by preheating an oven to 350 degrees F. Lightly grease a cookie sheet.

In the bowl of an electric mixer, combine together brownie mix, eggs, cardamom, anise seed, mace, and coconut oil; mix until everything is well blended.

Stir in chocolate morsels and walnuts.

Drop the dough by rounded teaspoonfuls onto prepared cookie sheet. Bake for 10 to 12 minutes.

Remove to wire racks to cool completely before serving. Enjoy!

Silken Tofu Chocolate Pie

(Ready in about 2 hours 10 minutes | Servings 8)

Ingredients

2 cups chocolate morsels

1/3 cup coffee liqueur

1 ¾ cups silken tofu

1/2 teaspoon pure almond extract

1 teaspoon pure vanilla extract

1 tablespoon maple syrup

1 chocolate wafer pie crust

Directions

Microwave the chocolate and coffee liqueur together until the mixture is completely melted.

Replace the chocolate mixture to a blender or a food processor. Add the tofu, almond extract, vanilla extract, and maple syrup; blend until smooth.

Pour the filling into the wafer pie crust; refrigerate for 2 hours, or until the pie is set.

Coconut Vanilla Macaroons

(Ready in about 20 minutes | Servings 6)

Ingredients

2 ½ cups coconut, shredded

1/3 cup flour

1/2 cup sugar

A pinch of salt

2/3 cup sweetened condensed milk

1/2 teaspoon pure coconut extract

1 teaspoon vanilla extract

Directions

Begin by preheating your oven to 350 degrees F. Lightly grease a baking pan with non-stick cooking spray.

Combine coconut, flour, sugar and salt together in a mixing bowl.

Add condensed milk, coconut extract, and vanilla. Mix with a spoon until everything is well incorporated.

Drop by teaspoonful onto lightly greased baking pan, lined with baking paper.

Bake 13 to 15 minutes or till golden. Transfer to a wire rack in order to cool before serving.

Chip and Easy Microwave Brownies

(Ready in about 10 minutes | Servings 6)

Ingredients

1 cup white sugar

1/2 cup butter, softened

2 eggs, lightly beaten

1 teaspoon vanilla extract

1 teaspoon cardamom

1/2 teaspoon ground mace

1/2 cup all-purpose flour

1/2 cup cocoa powder

Table sugar, as garnish

Directions

In a mixing bowl, cream white sugar and softened butter together. Stir in eggs, vanilla, cardamom, and ground mace; mix to combine well.

Stir in the flour and cocoa powder; add to the butter mixture. Mix again.

Lightly grease a pie pan; coat it with table sugar. Pour cake mixture into prepared pie pan.

Microwave your cake about 5 minutes. Allow to rest on a wire rack until cool. Sprinkle with some extra sugar if desired and serve.

Tropical Fruit Salad

(Ready in about 15 minutes | Servings 6)

Ingredients

1 cup banana, sliced

2 cups pineapple chunks

1 cup mango chunks

1 cup apple, cored, peeled and diced

1 tablespoon lemon juice

1 tablespoon brown sugar

1/2 teaspoon grated nutmeg

1/4 teaspoon ground cardamom

1/4 teaspoon ginger

Directions

In a salad bowl, combine together the banana, pineapple, mango, and apple. Drizzle with lemon juice.

Next, toss with sugar, nutmeg, cardamom, and ginger. Cover and place in a refrigerator for about 1 hour.

Sprinkle with chopped nuts, if desired. Enjoy!

Blueberry Jam Crumb Cake

(Ready in about 40 minutes | Servings 12)

Ingredients

1 cup biscuit mix

1 cup flour

1/2 teaspoon baking soda

1 teaspoon baking powder

1 tablespoon shortening

1 cup quick-cooking oats

3/4 cup dark brown sugar, packed

1 stick butter

1 cup blueberry jam

Directions

Begin by preheating an oven to 400 degrees F. Grease a square baking pan with non-stick cooking spray.

Mix together first 7 ingredients in a large-sized bowl. Cut in butter, using pastry blender until your mixture is crumbly.

Press half of the mixture into the prepared baking pan. Spread blueberry jam over the mixture.

Top with another half of crumbly mixture; press gently.

Bake about 30 minutes; cool completely before slicing and serving.

Double Layer Pudding Pie

(Ready in about 40 minutes | Servings 12)

Ingredients

1 ¼ cups milk

2 (3.5-ounce) packages chocolate flavor instant pudding mix

1 ½ cups yellow whipped topping

1 graham cracker pie crust

Strawberry halves, as garnish

Directions

In a medium-sized mixing bowl, beat the milk with pudding mix and 1 cup of whipped topping.

Then, spread the mixture evenly onto the pie crust.

Spread remaining 1/2 cup of whipped topping over pudding layer.

Garnish with strawberry halves. Enjoy chilled!

Insanely Good Butter Rolls

(Ready in about 25 minutes | Servings 16)

Ingredients

2 (8-ounce) cans crescent rolls

1 cup milk

1/2 cup buttermilk

2 cups powdered sugar

1/2 cup butter, melted

Directions

Start by preheating an oven to 350 degrees F.

Cut the dough into 8 rolls. Transfer the rolls to a baking dish.

In a bowl, combine milk, buttermilk, powdered sugar, and butter; mix with a wire whisk until the mixture is uniform and frothy. Pour this mixture over rolls.

Bake till your rolls are golden brown or about 15 minutes. Serve immediately or at room temperature. Enjoy!

Banana Cake with Cheese Frosting

(Ready in about 1 hour 15 minutes | Servings 16)

Ingredients

3 ripe bananas, mashed

1 tablespoon fresh lemon juice

3 cups all-purpose flour

1/2 teaspoon baking powder

1 teaspoon baking soda

3/4 cup butter, softened

2 ¼ cups sugar

1/4 teaspoon grated nutmeg

1/2 teaspoon ground cinnamon

3 eggs, lightly beaten

1 teaspoon pure vanilla extract

1 ½ cups buttermilk

For the Frosting:

1 stick butter, softened

1 cup cream cheese, softened

3 ½ cups powdered sugar

For the Garnish:

Pecans, toasted and chopped

Directions

Begin by preheating an oven to 275 degrees F. Then, butter and flour a baking pan.

In a bowl, combine bananas with the lemon juice; reserve. In a separate mixing bowl, mix flour, baking powder, and baking soda; reserve.

In another large-sized mixing bowl, cream 3/4 cup of butter with 2 ¼ cups sugar, nutmeg and cinnamon until the mixture is light and fluffy.

Next, beat in the eggs, one at a time; add vanilla extract and mix to combine well.

Stir in the flour mixture alternately with the 1 ½ cups of buttermilk. Stir in banana mixture. Beat the mixture until everything is well incorporated.

Pour your banana batter into prepared baking pan; bake for 1 hour or until a stick pierced in center comes out clean.

Transfer to a freezer for 45 minutes.

To prepare the frosting, cream the butter and cream cheese until uniform and smooth. Add powdered sugar; then, beat on low speed until the mixture is well combined; turn to high speed and beat for 1 minute more.

Spread the frosting on cooled cake. Afterwards, sprinkle chopped pecans over top of the frosting. Enjoy!

Lemon Meringue Pie

(Ready in about 20 minutes | Servings 8)

Ingredients

1 ½ cups sugar

1/2 cup cornstarch

1 ½ cups water

3 egg yolks

1 teaspoon ground cardamom

1/2 teaspoon allspice

Juice of 2 fresh lemons

1/2 teaspoon vanilla extract

1/4 teaspoon ground mace

2 tablespoons butter, softened

1 pie crust, baked

For the Meringue:

3 egg whites

6 tablespoons sugar

A pinch of salt

Directions

In a microwavable bowl, add 1 ½ cups sugar, cornstarch, and water. Stir to combine; microwave on high for 5 minutes, stirring once.

Add the egg yolks to hot mixture. Add cardamom, allspice, lemon juice, vanilla, and ground mace. Cook for about 3 minutes on 70% power.

Add butter and stir to combine; pour into baked pie crust. Allow to cool.

To make the Meringue: In a food processor, blend 3 egg whites, adding gradually 6 tablespoons of sugar; add the salt.

Bake at 350 degrees F until it's golden. Serve at room temperature.

Summer Party Strawberry Pie

(Ready in about 20 minutes | Servings 8)

Ingredients

3/4 cup granulated sugar

2 tablespoons cornstarch

1/2 teaspoon anise seed

1 teaspoon vanilla

1 ½ cups water

1 (6-ounce) package strawberry gelatin dessert

4 cups fresh strawberries, halved

1 graham cracker crust

Directions

In a large-sized saucepan, bring the sugar, cornstarch, anise seed, vanilla, and water to a boil; cook until the mixture is thickened.

Add strawberry gelatin and stir until everything is well mixed.

Let mixture cool down for a few minutes. Add the strawberries to the cracker crust.

Pour the mixture over strawberries; refrigerate till gelatin mixture is solid. Serve chilled and enjoy!

HEALTHY RECIPES

Sugar-Free Butter Cookies

(Ready in about 20 minutes | Servings 8)

Ingredients

1/2 cup coconut flour

1 ½ cups almond flour

2 eggs

1/4 cup coconut oil

1/2 cup ghee

4 tablespoons raw honey

Directions

Begin by preheating an oven to 325 degrees F. Coat a cookie sheet with parchment paper.

In a large-sized mixing bowl, combine together all the above ingredients. Mix until everything is well blended.

Bake about 12 minutes. Transfer to a cooling rack before serving. Place on a nice serving platter, dust with icing sugar if desired, and serve.

Chocolate Dream Cupcakes

(Ready in about 25 minutes | Servings 12)

Ingredients

Non-stick cooking spray

1/4 cup coconut flour

3/4 cup almond flour

3 large-sized eggs

2/3 cup canola oil

1/4 teaspoon grated nutmeg

1/2 teaspoon ground cinnamon

4 tablespoons raw honey

2 tablespoons of sugar

A pinch of salt

2/3 cup cocoa powder

1/2 teaspoon pure hazelnut extract

1/2 teaspoon baking powder

1 teaspoon baking soda

Chocolate shavings, as garnish

Directions

Preheat an oven to 350 degrees F. Lightly grease a muffin tin with non-stick cooking spray.

In a mixing bowl, combine together all the above ingredients, except chocolate shavings. Mix until everything is well blended.

Pour the batter into 12 muffin cups.

Bake in the preheated oven for about 15 minutes. Allow to stand on a cooling rack about 10 minutes. Then, transfer to a serving platter. Sprinkle with chocolate shavings and serve!

Healthy Sweet Banana Bread

(Ready in about 10 minutes | Servings 8)

Ingredients

1/3 cup almond flour

1 tablespoon coconut oil, melted

1 tablespoon ghee

1 small-sized ripe banana, mashed

4 tablespoons agave syrup

1/2 teaspoon allspice

1/2 teaspoon baking powder

1/8 teaspoon salt

1 teaspoon pure vanilla extract

Powdered sugar, for garnish

Directions

Mix all the above ingredients together, except the powdered sugar.

Microwave the mixture for about 2 minutes on high.

Dust with powdered sugar and serve.

Low Fat Chocolate and Coconut Cupcakes

(Ready in about 35 minutes | Servings 6)

Ingredients

1/4 cup honey

1/2 cup coconut cream

1/4 cup ghee

1 cup cocoa powder

1/2 teaspoon grated nutmeg

1/2 teaspoon ground cinnamon

Colored coconut flakes, as garnish

Directions

Place the honey, coconut cream, and ghee in a mixing bowl. Then, melt over a bowl of hot water.

Add the cocoa powder, grated nutmeg, and cinnamon. Mix until everything is well incorporated.

Next, spoon the mixture into 6 muffin cups and freeze for 25 minutes. Garnish with colored coconut flakes.

You can keep leftovers in the fridge. Enjoy!

Easiest and Healthiest Pumpkin Pie

(Ready in about 10 minutes | Servings 1)

Ingredients

6 tablespoons canned pumpkin purée

3 tablespoons coconut oil

3 tablespoons cocoa powder

1/4 teaspoon ground cloves

1/2 teaspoon ground cinnamon

1/2 teaspoon dry grated ginger

1/4 teaspoon grated nutmeg

1 tablespoon agave nectar

Directions

Place all the above ingredients into a microwaveable bowl; microwave for 45 seconds on high. Then, transfer to a blender.

Process until the mixture is creamy, uniform, and smooth.

Serve chilled and enjoy.

Family Date Delight

(Ready in about 15 minutes | Servings 4)

Ingredients

1/2 cup ghee

1 cup coconut butter

24 dates, pitted

1 teaspoon ground cinnamon

Directions

Begin by melting the ghee and coconut butter in the microwave. Melt in order to soften the mixture and make it easier to blend.

Slice your dates so that they're open.

Fill each date with melted butter mixture; sprinkle with ground cinnamon. Arrange on a serving platter; serve.

Romantic Banana Pancakes

(Ready in about 45 minutes | Servings 2)

Ingredients

2 ripe bananas, peeled

2 medium-sized eggs, slightly beaten

1/2 teaspoon ground cinnamon

Coconut oil, for pan

Maple syrup, as garnish (optional)

Hulled strawberries, as garnish (optional)

Directions

To make the batter: Put the bananas, eggs, and cinnamon into your blender or a food processor.

Heat the coconut oil in a pan over medium heat. Pour 1/2 of the batter in a pan. Fry the pancake approximately 10 minutes.

Then, flip the pancake and cook another 10 minutes on the other side.

Next, prepare the second pancake according to the same procedure. Slide the pancake onto a serving platter.

Serve with maple syrup and strawberries if desired and enjoy!

Party Banana Coconut Balls

(Ready in about 25 minutes | Servings 6)

Ingredients

1 large-sized ripe banana, mashed

2 cups coconut, shredded

1 tablespoon agave nectar

1 tablespoon ghee, softened

1 tablespoon coconut oil, softened

1 teaspoon pure coconut extract

Colored coconut flakes, as garnish

Directions

Start by preheating an oven to 250 degrees F.

To make the batter, in a mixing bowl, combine together all the above ingredients, except colored coconut flakes.

Using your hands, shape the batter into 12 balls.

Then, bake in the preheated oven at 250 degrees F for 15 minutes. Sprinkle with colored coconut flakes.

Arrange on a nice serving platter, serve and enjoy!

Ginger Pecan Cookies

(Ready in about 25 minutes | Servings 6)

Ingredients

1 tablespoon flax seeds	1 teaspoon ground cinnamon
1 tablespoon chia seed	1/2 teaspoon grated nutmeg
2 cups whole pecans	1/2 teaspoon ground cloves
1/4 cup coconut oil	2 tablespoons grated ginger
2 medium-sized egg, lightly beaten	6 tablespoons honey
A pinch of salt	

Directions

Start by preheating an oven to 350 degrees F. Line a cookie sheet with a parchment paper or a silicone baking mat.

Add flax seeds, chia seeds, and whole pecans to a food processor or a blender. Process until the pecans are coarsely chopped. Transfer to a mixing bowl.

Next, add the remaining ingredients to the mixing bowl. Mix to combine well.

Shape the balls with your hands; flatten them with the bottom of a glass. Transfer to the cookie sheet and place in the preheated oven.

Bake about 15 minutes. Transfer to a serving platter and dust with icing sugar if desired. Enjoy!

Yummy Puffy Cookies

(Ready in about 20 minutes | Servings 6)

Ingredients

3 large-sized egg whites

2/3 cup almond flour

2 tablespoons agave nectar

4 tablespoons honey

1/4 teaspoon grated nutmeg

1 teaspoon pure almond extract

Directions

Begin by preheating an oven to 350 degrees F. Line a cookie sheet with a parchment paper or a silicone baking mat.

Then, beat the egg whites using an electric mixer on high speed; beat until stiff peaks form.

Fold in the rest of the above ingredients. Mix until everything is well combined.

Drop 12 small dollops of the mixture onto a cookie sheet. Bake until the cookies become slightly golden on top or about 12 minutes.

Transfer to a cooling rack in order to cool completely before serving time. Enjoy!

Raw Walnut and Coconut Cakes

(Ready in about 40 minutes | Servings 4)

Ingredients

2 tablespoons ghee, melted

1 tablespoon agave nectar

1 tablespoon honey

1/2 cup coconut, shredded

1/2 cup walnuts, ground

Chocolate chips, as garnish

Directions

To make the batter: In a mixing bowl, combine together all the above ingredients. Mix until everything is well combined.

Shape the batter into eight cookies by using your hands.

Set in a fridge at least 30 minutes. Then, transfer to a serving platter and serve.

Pecan Chocolate Treat

(Ready in about 20 minutes | Servings 8)

Ingredients

2 cups pecans

1 tablespoon hemp seeds

1 tablespoon chia seeds

1/2 teaspoon grated nutmeg

1/2 teaspoon ground cinnamon

1/4 cup shredded coconut, unsweetened

1 large-sized egg, slightly beaten

1/4 cup coconut oil

3 tablespoons honey

1/4 cocoa powder

A pinch of salt

1/2 teaspoon baking powder

1/2 teaspoon baking soda

Directions

Begin by preheating an oven to 350 degrees F.

Process the pecans, hemp seeds, and chia seeds in a blender or a food processor. Transfer to a mixing bowl.

To make the batter: Add the rest of the ingredients and mix until everything is well blended.

Shape the batter into eight cookies. Bake for about 12 minutes. Enjoy!

Refreshing Coffee Crème

(Ready in about 30 minutes | Servings 2)

Ingredients

1/4 cup cocoa powder

1/2 teaspoon cinnamon

1/2 teaspoon dry grated ginger

1 tablespoon coconut oil, melted

2 teaspoons coffee beans, ground

2 tablespoons agave syrup

6 tablespoons coconut cream

Directions

In a mixing bowl, combine all the above ingredients till everything is well combined.

Pour the mixture into two small-sized cups.

Next, set in a fridge at least 20 minutes before serving time.

Garnish with coffee beans if desired. Enjoy!

Flavorful Pudding Pie

(Ready in about 4 hours 45 minutes | Servings 10)

Ingredients

For the Crust:

30 chocolate wafers

1/2 cup dark chocolate, melted

1/2 teaspoon ground cinnamon

1/4 teaspoon grated nutmeg

1 tablespoon coconut oil

For the Filling:

3/4 cup brown sugar

1/4 cup corn flour

1/4 cup cocoa powder

1/2 teaspoon anise seed

A pinch of salt

1 ¾ cups milk

2 large-sized egg yolks

1/2 cup dark chocolate, finely chopped

1 tablespoon rum

For the Garnish:

1/2 cup fresh strawberries

10 tablespoon whipped topping

Directions

To make the crust, pulse chocolate wafers in a food processor till finely ground.

Add 1/2 cup dark chocolate, cinnamon, nutmeg, and coconut oil. Then, process until the mixture is well blended. Press into a pie plate and freeze approximately 15 minutes.

To make the filling, in a large-sized saucepan, combine brown sugar, corn flour, cocoa powder, anise seed, and salt; cook over medium-low flame, stirring with a wire whisk.

Add half of milk and egg yolks; stir until the mixture is fluffy and smooth. Next, add the remaining milk.

Decrease heat to medium. Continue cooking over medium heat for 5 minutes, stirring frequently. Then, turn off the heat. Add 1/2 cup of dark chocolate. Add rum and stir again.

Pour prepared filling into cooled crust. Set in a refrigerator about 4 hours. Divide among dessert bowls; garnish with strawberries and whipped topping; serve.

Grandma's Chocolate Cake

(Ready in about 30 minutes + chilling time | Servings 20)

Ingredients

Non-stick cooking spray

2 teaspoons flour

2 cups pastry flour

2 cups sugar

1/2 teaspoon baking powder

1 teaspoon baking soda

1/2 teaspoon grated nutmeg

1 teaspoon ground cinnamon

A pinch of salt

3/4 cup water

1/2 cup butter

1/2 cup unsweetened cocoa powder

1/2 cup buttermilk

2 large-sized eggs

6 tablespoons butter

1/3 cup fat-free milk

3 cups powdered sugar

1/4 cup almonds, chopped and toasted

Directions

Begin by preheating your oven to 375 degrees F. Then, treat the inside of a 13 x 9-inch baking pan with non-stick cooking spray; dust with 2 teaspoons of flour.

Sift 2 cups of flour into a mixing bowl; level with a knife. Add sugar, baking powder, baking soda, grated nutmeg, ground cinnamon, and salt; stir with a wire whisk.

In a saucepan, combine water, 1/2 cup butter, and 1/4 cup of cocoa powder; bring to a boil and stir frequently. Add this wet mixture to the flour mixture.

To prepare the batter: beat your mixture with an electric mixer at medium speed. Add buttermilk and eggs; beat until everything is well combined.

Pour the batter into the greased baking pan. Bake about 22 minutes. Transfer to a wire rack.

In a saucepan, combine together 6 tablespoons butter, fat-free milk, and remaining 1/4 cup cocoa; bring to a boil, stirring frequently.

Remove from the heat and add powdered sugar. Stir to combine. Sprinkle your cake with almonds. Serve chilled and enjoy.

Coconut-Mango Ice Cream

(Ready in about 20 minutes | Servings 2)

Ingredients

1/4 cup coconut cream

1 cup mango chunks

1/4 cup coconut, shredded

1/2 tablespoon orange juice

1 teaspoon ginger

2 tablespoons raw honey

Directions

Add all the above ingredients to a blender or a food processor.

Blend until the mixture is creamy and uniform.

Divide among two serving bowls and sprinkle with some extra coconut if desired. Serve chilled.

Best Coconut Macaroons Ever

(Ready in about 20 minutes | Servings 8)

Ingredients

4 large-sized egg whites

3 cups unsweetened coconut, shredded

3 tablespoons agave nectar

1/4 cup cocoa powder

1/4 teaspoon allspice

1/2 teaspoon grated ginger

1/4 teaspoon salt

1 teaspoon pure coconut extract

Directions

Begin by preheating an oven to 350 degrees F. Coat a cookie sheet with parchment paper.

Using an electric mixer, beat the egg whites until stiff peaks form.

Add the rest of the above ingredients and mix to combine well.

Bake for about 15 minutes. Transfer to a serving platter; serve.

Vegan Chocolate Pudding

(Ready in about 9 hours 10 minutes | Servings 2)

Ingredients

2 tablespoons cocoa powder

1 cup almond milk

1/3 cup chia seeds

1 tablespoon unsweetened coconut, shredded

1/4 teaspoon ground cinnamon

Directions

In a mixing bowl, combine together all the above ingredients. Mix until everything is well blended.

Then, refrigerate the mixture for about 9 hours or overnight.

Divide among two serving bowls and garnish with chocolate sprinkles if desired. Enjoy!

Sugar-Free Cupcakes

(Ready in about 30 minutes | Servings 6)

Ingredients

1/2 cup almond meal

1/2 teaspoon baking soda

1/4 teaspoon baking powder

1/2 teaspoon allspice

A pinch of salt

1/2 cup cocoa powder, unsweetened

1 teaspoon espresso powder

3 packets of stevia

1 tablespoon ghee, melted

4 teaspoons coconut oil, melted

1/2 cup applesauce

2 medium-sized eggs, lightly beaten

1 teaspoon pure coconut extract

1 teaspoon pure hazelnut extract

For the Frosting:

3 tablespoons coconut oil, at room temperature

1/4 cup peanut butter

1/4 cup unsweetened cocoa powder

2 packets of Stevia

Directions

Begin by preheating an oven to 375 degrees F. Then, coat a muffin pan with 6 paper cups.

In a mixing bowl, combine the almond meal, baking soda, baking powder, allspice, salt, cocoa powder, espresso powder, and Stevia. Mix to combine well and reserve.

In another mixing bowl, combine the ghee, coconut oil, applesauce, eggs, coconut extract, and hazelnut extract.

To prepare the batter: Pour the wet ingredients into the dry ingredients; stir until the mixture is well blended.

Fill the muffin pan with the batter. Bake about 20 minutes, or until a wooden stick comes out clean. Allow your cupcakes to cool in a wire rack.

Meanwhile, prepare the frosting, by mixing all the frosting ingredients.

Spread the frosting on each cupcake and serve.

Honey Pecan Toffee

(Ready in about 15 minutes + chilling time | Servings 8)

Ingredients

2 teaspoons ghee

1 teaspoon coconut oil, melted

1/4 cup honey

1/2 cup pecans

1/4 teaspoon ground cinnamon

1/4 teaspoon salt

Directions

In a pot, combine the ghee, coconut oil and honey over medium heat. Stir constantly.

Add the pecans, cinnamon, and salt.

Pour onto a piece of parchment paper and set in a refrigerator. Serve chilled.

Summer Coffee Truffles

(Ready in about 5 hours 10 minutes | Servings 2)

Ingredients

1/2 cup coconut oil

3 tablespoons cocoa powder

1 tablespoon ground coffee

1/4 teaspoon grated ginger

3 tablespoons ground walnuts

1 tablespoon shredded coconut

1 teaspoon raw honey

Directions

Melt the coconut oil in a microwave. Transfer to a mixing bowl. Add the rest of the ingredients and mix to combine well.

Freeze in an ice-cube tray at least 5 hours.

Defrost at room temperature before serving and enjoy.

Vanilla Berry Jelly

(Ready in about 4 hours 10 minutes | Servings 2)

Ingredients

1 cup raspberries

1 cup blueberries

1 teaspoon pure vanilla extract

2 tablespoons gelatin powder

1 cup cold water

Directions

In a food processor or a blender, purée the raspberries and blueberries. Stir in vanilla and mix to combine. Transfer to the cups.

Put gelatin powder into a large-sized microwave-safe bowl; next, add cold water. Stir until the mixture is well combined.

Then, transfer the bowl to the microwave; heat about 1 minute on high; mix well.

Pour the gelatin mixture into the cups with the fruits; mix to combine well. Then, set in a fridge about 4 hours.

Serve chilled and enjoy.

Almond Pound Cake

(Ready in about 1 hour | Servings 8)

Ingredients

3 cups almond flour

1/3 cup whey protein powder

1 teaspoon baking soda

1 teaspoon baking powder

1/2 cup coconut oil, at room temperature

3 eggs, slightly beaten

1 teaspoon lemon zest

1/2 teaspoon allspice

| 1 tablespoon pure almond extract | 1/2 cup brown sugar |
| 4 tablespoons honey | 1/2 cup milk |

Directions

Begin by preheating an oven to 300 degrees F. Then, treat the inside of a loaf pan with non-stick cooking spray.

To make the batter: In a mixing bowl, combine all the above ingredients together.

Pour the batter into the greased loaf pan. Bake about 1 hour or till the top turns golden brown.

Transfer to a wire rack. Allow to cool completely before cutting and serving.

Banana Almond Parfait

(Ready in about 20 minutes | Servings 4)

Ingredients

6 tablespoons brown sugar	2 large-sized ripe bananas, cut into chunks
2 tablespoons apple juice	2 cups Greek yogurt
1 tablespoon butter, melted	1/4 cup almonds, chopped
A pinch of salt	

Directions

In a nonstick skillet, combine together the sugar, apple juice, butter, and salt. Cook over medium-low flame for about 3 minutes, till the mixture starts to bubble.

Add bananas to the skillet; cook 2 more minutes.

Divide Greek yogurt among 4 parfait glasses. Then add the banana mixture. Top with chopped almonds and serve.

Berry and Pineapple Parfait

(Ready in about 15 minutes | Servings 4)

Ingredients

2 cups berry yogurt

1 cup fresh raspberries

1/4 cup fresh strawberries

1 ½ cups pineapple chunks

1 teaspoon ground cinnamon

Directions

Layer the berry yogurt in the parfait glasses.

Then, add raspberries and strawberries.

Top with pineapple chunks. Sprinkle each parfait glass with ground cinnamon and serve chilled.

White Chocolate Cranberry Cookies

(Ready in about 35 minutes | Servings 6)

Ingredients

1 cup flour

1/4 cup wheat germ

1/2 teaspoon baking powder

1/2 teaspoon baking soda

1/2 teaspoon dry ground ginger

1/4 teaspoon salt

1 large-sized egg, slightly beaten

3/4 cup packed brown sugar

1/3 cup coconut oil

1 teaspoon pure coconut extract

1/2 cup quick-cooking oats

2 ounces white chocolate, chopped

1/3 cup dried cranberries

1/2 teaspoon ground cinnamon

1/4 teaspoon ground cloves

1/4 cup crystallized ginger

Directions

Begin by preheating an oven to 375 degrees F.

In a medium-sized mixing bowl, combine the flour, wheat germ, baking powder, baking soda, ground ginger, and salt.

In another mixing bowl, combine the egg, brown sugar, coconut oil, and coconut extract.

Next, make the dough, adding the dry ingredients to the wet ingredients; stir until everything is well combined. Stir in oats, white chocolate, dried cranberries, cinnamon, cloves, and crystallized ginger; mix to combine.

Drop the dough by rounded tablespoonfuls onto baking sheets.

Bake the cookies about 10 minutes, or until they are barely golden around the edges.

Place the cookies on a wire rack to cool completely before serving.

Creamy Cherry Dessert with Walnuts

(Ready in about 15 minutes | Servings 2)

Ingredients

1 cup cherries, pitted

4 tablespoons ricotta

1/4 teaspoon ground cinnamon

1/2 teaspoon anise seed

2 tablespoons walnuts, chopped and toasted

Directions

Heat cherries in the microwave about 2 minutes. Then, place the warm cherries in the dessert bowls.

Top with ricotta. Sprinkle with cinnamon, anise seed, and walnuts. Serve.

Easy and Healthy Tiramisu

(Ready in about 15 minutes | Servings 6)

Ingredients

1/2 cup ricotta cheese

2 tablespoons sugar

1/4 teaspoon ground cinnamon

1/4 teaspoon ground mace

1/2 teaspoon pure almond extract

12 spongy ladyfingers

4 tablespoons strong coffee

2 tablespoons dark chocolate, melted

Directions

Add ricotta cheese, sugar, cinnamon, mace and almond extract to a mixing bowl.

Place 6 ladyfingers in a small-sized loaf pan. Drizzle with 2 tablespoons of coffee.

Then, place the ricotta mixture over the ladyfingers. Then, place another layer of 6 ladyfingers.

Drizzle with the remaining 2 tablespoons of coffee. Then, drizzle with chocolate. Set in a refrigerator for about 30 minutes. Serve chilled.

Winter Orange Dessert

(Ready in about 15 minutes | Servings 6)

Ingredients

4 navel oranges

3 tablespoons lemon juice

1 tablespoon agave nectar

1/4 teaspoon ground cinnamon

Directions

Remove rind and white pith from the oranges with a sharp knife.

Cut the oranges into slices and place them on four serving plates.

Drizzle with lemon juice and agave nectar. Sprinkle with ground cinnamon. Serve.

Cocoa and Coconut Banana Bites

(Ready in about 10 minutes | Servings 4)

Ingredients

4 teaspoons cocoa powder

4 teaspoons coconut flakes toasted

2 small bananas, sliced

1 teaspoon fresh orange juice

Directions

Place cocoa powder in a shallow bowl. In another shallow bowl, place the coconut flakes.

Dip each banana slice in the cocoa; then, dip in the coconut flakes. Drizzle with orange juice.

Arrange on a nice serving platter. Serve.

Spring Berry Mousse

(Ready in about 2 hours 25 minutes | Servings 6)

Ingredients

1 cup mixed berries, finely chopped

8 tablespoons sugar

5 tablespoons water

3/4 teaspoon gelatin

2 large-sized egg whites, slightly beaten

1/2 teaspoon pure vanilla extract

1/2 cup heavy whipping cream

Directions

Add mixed berries and 1 tablespoon of sugar in the bowl of a food processor. Then, process until smooth and uniform.

Pour 2 tablespoons of water into a mixing bowl; then, add the gelatin. Allow to sit about 5 minutes.

In a saucepan, combine together 6 tablespoons sugar and the remaining 3 tablespoons water over medium-high heat; bring to a boil. Continue cooking for 4 minutes.

Add slightly beaten egg whites to gelatin mixture; beat with an electric mixer at high speed. Finally, add remaining 1 tablespoon sugar; continue beating till soft peaks form.

Slowly add sugar syrup to the egg white mixture; continue beating until stiff peaks form. Add pure vanilla extract; stir again.

Transfer the cream to the bowl and beat with an electric mixer at high speed. Add 1/4 of the mixture to heavy whipping cream. Add the remaining egg white mixture. Next, fold in berry mixture.

Set in a refrigerator for at least 2 hours before serving.

Summer Fluffy Nutty Pie

(Ready in about 20 minutes + chilling time | Servings 20)

Ingredients

1 cup powdered sugar

1 cup reduced-fat peanut butter

1 cup cream cheese, softened

1 (14-ounce) can fat-free milk

1 ½ cups fat-free whipped topping

2 tablespoons ground walnuts

1/4 teaspoon allspice

1/2 teaspoon pure almond extract

2 (6-ounce) reduced-fat graham cracker crusts

2 tablespoons fat-free chocolate syrup

Directions

In a large bowl, combine together powdered sugar, peanut butter, and cream cheese.

Cream with an electric mixer at medium speed. Add canned fat-free milk; continue beating. Gently fold in fat-free whipped topping, ground walnuts, allspice, and almond extract.

Next, divide the mixture between two graham cracker crusts. Allow to chill in a fridge overnight or for 8 to 9 hours.

Drizzle with chocolate syrup, cut into slices and serve.

Heart-Healthy Fruit Dessert

(Ready in about 40 minutes | Servings 6)

Ingredients

1 tablespoon agave nectar

1 tablespoon cornstarch

1 cup fresh pineapple juice

1/4 teaspoon pure coconut extract

1 cup fresh blueberries

1/2 cup banana, thinly sliced

6 sponge cake dessert shells

Shredded coconut, as garnish

Directions

In a small-sized skillet, combine together the agave nectar and cornstarch. Add the pineapple juice and cook for 1 minute, bringing to a boil; make sure to stir constantly. Set aside in order to cool completely.

To make the fruit sauce, transfer cold mixture to a large-sized bowl; add coconut extract, blueberries, and banana slices; stir gently to combine. Allow to sit in a refrigerator at least 30 minutes.

Spoon prepared fruit sauce over sponge cake dessert shells. Sprinkle with shredded coconut as garnish. Serve and enjoy!

Fudgy Creamy Brownies

(Ready in about 40 minutes | Servings 16)

Ingredients

Non-stick cooking spray

3/4 cup sugar

1/4 cup stick butter, softened

1 large egg white

1 large-sized egg

1 tablespoon pure almond extract

1/2 cup flour

1/2 teaspoon baking soda

1/2 teaspoon baking powder

1/4 teaspoon grated nutmeg

1/4 teaspoon ground cinnamon

1/4 cup cocoa powder

1 cup cream cheese, at room temperature

1/4 cup honey

3 tablespoons low-fat milk

Directions

Begin by preheating an oven to 350 degrees F. Lightly grease a baking dish with non-stick cooking spray.

Using an electric mixer, cream the sugar and butter at medium speed until fluffy. Then, add egg white, egg, and almond extract; beat until everything is well incorporated and combined.

Gradually and slowly add flour, baking soda, baking powder, nutmeg, cinnamon, and cocoa powder.

Pour the batter into prepared baking dish.

Next, combine together the cream cheese and honey; beat with a mixer at high speed until the mixture is creamy and smooth. Gradually pour in the milk.

Spread cream cheese mixture over cocoa mixture in the baking dish; swirl together using the tip of a knife.

Bake in the preheated oven for 30 minutes. Transfer to a wire rack to cool completely before slicing and serving.

Frozen Creamy Pie

(Ready in about 45 minutes + chilling time | Servings 10)

Ingredients

Non-stick cooking spray

1 ½ cups chocolate graham cracker crumbs

6 tablespoons brown sugar

2 large egg whites, lightly beaten

1 ¼ cups milk

2/3 cup reduced-fat peanut butter

1/2 cup fat-free cream cheese, at room temperature

1 cup fat-free whipped topping

3 tablespoons almonds, toasted and finely chopped

1/4 cup chocolate sprinkles

Directions

Begin by preheating your oven to 350 degrees F. Lightly grease a pie plate with non-stick cooking spray.

In a mixing bowl, combine together graham cracker crumbs, 3 tablespoons sugar, and beaten egg whites.

Press the mixture into the bottom of greased pie plate. Then, prick your pie crust with a fork. Bake approximately 10 minutes. Allow to cool on a wire rack.

Combine milk and remaining 3 tablespoons of brown sugar in a saucepan over medium-low heat. Cook until sugar dissolves or about 2 minutes, stirring often.

Transfer the mixture to a large-sized mixing bowl. Add peanut butter and place in a fridge for 30 minutes.

In a separate large-sized bowl, place cream cheese; beat with an electric mixer at medium speed. Add chilled milk and brown sugar mixture and continue beating on low speed until everything is well blended.

Then, fold in fat-free whipped topping; pour mixture into pie crust. Place the pie in a freezer for 8 to 9 hours or overnight. Scatter the almonds on top. Garnish with chocolate sprinkles and serve chilled.

Crispy Streusel Cookies

(Ready in about 30 minutes | Servings 16)

Ingredients

1 (16.5-ounce) package sugar cookie dough, frozen

1/4 cup brown sugar

1/4 cup walnuts, finely chopped

1/2 teaspoon ground cloves

3/4 teaspoon ground cinnamon

1/2 teaspoon pure vanilla extract

Directions

Begin by preheating an oven to 350 degrees F; then, place the rack in center of your oven. Line two cookie sheets with parchment paper.

Place the sugar cookie dough on cutting board. Cut the cookie dough into 32 slices. Transfer to the cookie sheets.

To make the streusel: In a medium-sized mixing bowl, combine together brown sugar, chopped walnuts, cloves, cinnamon, pure vanilla extract, and nutmeg.

Top cookies with prepared streusel. Bake approximately 12 minutes or until the edges of your cookies have browned. Transfer to a wire rack to cool completely before serving. Enjoy!

Strawberry Pudding Cake

(Ready in about 1 hour 15 minutes | Servings 6)

Ingredients

Non-stick cooking spray

3/4 cup almond flour

3/4 cup gluten-free flour mix

1/4 teaspoon xanthan gum

2 teaspoons baking powder

1/4 teaspoon grated nutmeg

1/2 teaspoon ground cinnamon

A pinch of salt

2/3 cup soymilk

1/3 cup agave syrup

1/3 cup egg whites

2 cups frozen strawberries

1/4 cup granulated sugar

1 cup boiling water

Directions

Start by preheating your oven to 350 degrees F. Lightly oil a baking dish with non-stick cooking spray.

Combine the almond flour, GF flour, xanthan, baking powder, grated nutmeg, cinnamon, and salt. Mix on low speed until the mixture is creamy and uniform.

To prepare the batter: In another bowl, combine together soymilk, agave syrup, and egg whites; mix to combine well. Add this wet mixture to the dry mixture; mix well to combine.

Arrange the frozen strawberries on the bottom of the prepared baking dish. Pour the batter on top of the strawberries.

Then, sprinkle the granulated sugar on top of the batter. Pour the boiling water into the baking dish. Bake about 1 hour. Allow to cool slightly before cutting and serving. Serve.

Hot Bananas in Sauce

(Ready in about 15 minutes | Servings 4)

Ingredients

1 stick butter

1/2 cup brown sugar

1 ¼ cups heavy cream

1 teaspoon ground cinnamon

4 bananas, peeled and halved lengthwise

Directions

In a large-sized saucepan, melt the butter over medium flame. Stir in brown sugar; cook about 10 minutes, stirring constantly.

Gradually add heavy cream and cinnamon. Bring to a boil.

Then, turn the heat to low. Add the bananas and cook about 2 minutes or till they are heated. Serve warm and enjoy.

Cranberry-Almond Treats

(Ready in about 15 minutes | Servings 2)

Ingredients

8 tablespoons bittersweet chocolate chips

1/4 cup dried cranberries

1/4 cup slivered almonds

Directions

Microwave the chocolate chips until melted or about 1 minute.

Stir in cranberries and almonds; stir to combine well.

Drop 6 rounded tablespoons onto waxed or parchment paper. Set aside in a refrigerator for 5 minutes. Serve and enjoy!

Creamy Pomegranate and Banana Dessert

(Ready in about 10 minutes | Servings 2)

Ingredients

1 cup nonfat Greek yogurt

1 banana, sliced

1 cup pomegranate seeds

5-6 leaves fresh mint

Directions

Pour Greek yogurt into two dessert dishes.

Add the banana slices and pomegranate seeds.

Garnish with mint leaves and serve!

Creamy Fruit Salad

(Ready in about 15 minutes | Servings 8)

Ingredients

1 (14-ounce) can milk sweetened

1 cup whipped topping

1 (16-ounce) can cherry pie filling

2 cups peaches, cut into chunks

1 ½ cups miniature marshmallows

1/4 cup almonds, chopped

Directions

In a large-sized salad bowl, combine together the milk and whipped topping.

Then, stir in the cherry pie filling, peaches, and miniature marshmallows. Mix well to combine.

Divide among dessert bowls. Sprinkle with chopped almonds. Serve!

Yummiest Nutty Fruit Salad

(Ready in about 15 minutes | Servings 8)

Ingredients

1 (16-ounce) can strawberry pie filling

1 cup whipped topping

1 ½ cups canned milk sweetened

2 cups strawberries, halved

2 bananas, sliced

1 apple, cored and diced

1/2 cup golden raisins

1 ½ cups miniature marshmallows

1/4 cup pecans, chopped

Directions

Place all of the above ingredients into a large-sized bowl. Gently stir to combine well.

Divide the salad among eight dessert bowls. Sprinkle with some extra pecans if desired. Serve chilled and enjoy!

Amazing Tropical Sorbet

(Ready in about 2 hours 25 minutes | Servings 8)

Ingredients

1/2 cup almond milk

1/2 cup sugar

1 pineapple, cut into chunks

1/2 teaspoon almond extract

1/4 teaspoon ground cloves

1/2 teaspoon ground cinnamon

2 teaspoons lemon juice

Directions

In a heavy skillet, place together the almond milk and sugar; cook over medium-low flame; bring to a simmer for about 2 minutes. Turn off the heat and allow to cool for 20 minutes. Replace to a large bowl.

Purée the pineapple chunks in a food processor until smooth. Add the pineapple purée to the coconut milk mixture; mix to combine well. Add pure almond extract, cloves, cinnamon, and lemon juice.

Then refrigerate until chilled or about 1 hour.

Pour the chilled mixture into an ice cream maker and freeze it. Then place in a food processor and blend until smooth.

Pour into chilled dessert dishes and serve.

Raw Chocolate Oatmeal Cookies

(Ready in about 1 hour 15 minutes | Servings 8)

Ingredients

1/2 cup walnuts

1 cup raw rolled oats

1 tablespoon ghee

3 tablespoons agave nectar

1/2 teaspoon allspice

A pinch of salt

1 tablespoon coconut water

1/2 teaspoon pure almond extract

1/2 cup raw chocolate chips

Directions

Grind up the walnuts and half of the rolled oats in your food processor.

Next, add ghee, agave nectar, allspice, salt, coconut water. Add almond extract and remaining half of the rolled oats; pulse until everything is well combined.

Transfer to a refrigerator for 1 hour. After that, stir in raw chocolate chips.

Shape the batter into 16 cookies. Freeze the cookies in an airtight container. Serve chilled.

Frozen Yogurt and Coffee Dessert

(Ready in about 15 minutes | Servings 2)

Ingredients

1 cup vanilla frozen yogurt

1 teaspoon Kahlua coffee liqueur

1/4 teaspoon grated nutmeg

1/2 teaspoon anise seed

3 tablespoons hot espresso

Directions

Divide frozen yogurt among two chilled dessert dishes.

Add remaining ingredients. Serve.

Creamy Apple-Pear Delight

(Ready in about 15 minutes | Servings 6)

Ingredients

2 tablespoons butter, softened

1 apple, peeled, cored and cubed

1 pear, peeled, cored, and cubed

1 tablespoon lime juice

2 tablespoons brown sugar

2 tablespoons plain nonfat yogurt

18 mini phyllo shells

Directions

In a large-sized saucepan, melt butter over medium-low flame. Then, add apple, pear, lime juice, and 1 tablespoon of brown sugar. Cook about 7 minutes; toss often.

In a small-sized mixing bowl, combine together plain yogurt and the remaining 1 tablespoon of brown sugar.

Divide the fruit mixture among 18 mini phyllo shells. Then, top them with yogurt mixture.

Garnish with chopped nuts if desired. Serve and enjoy.

Ricotta Chocolate Sandwich Cookies

(Ready in about 15 minutes | Servings 6)

Ingredients

3/4 cup part-skim ricotta

1 ½ tablespoons orange marmalade

1 tablespoon honey

1 tablespoon shaved dark chocolate

1/4 teaspoon pure coconut extract

16 ginger thins

Directions

In a small-sized bowl, stir together ricotta, orange marmalade, and honey; stir until everything is well combined.

Fold in shaved chocolate and coconut extract.

Arrange eight ginger thins on a rimmed baking sheet. Spoon the prepared ricotta mixture onto each cookie. Top with the remaining eight ginger thins.

Then, freeze at least 1 hour or until the cookies are set. Serve chilled and enjoy.

Marshmallow Red Velvet Cupcakes

(Ready in about 25 minutes | Servings 10)

Ingredients

1/2 (18.25-ounce) box red velvet cake mix

1/2 cup water

3 tablespoons applesauce

1/4 teaspoon grated nutmeg

1/2 teaspoon ground cinnamon

1 large-sized egg white

1 large-sized egg

1 cup marshmallow fluff

Directions

Begin by preheating an oven to 325 degrees F.

In a mixing bowl, combine red velvet cake mix, water, applesauce, nutmeg, cinnamon, egg white, and whole egg white and beat until smooth.

Pour prepared batter into wrapper-lined mini-muffin tins; bake about 17 minutes.

Next, place on a wire rack in order to cool completely. Garnish with marshmallow fluff and serve.

Date and Cashew Rice Pudding

(Ready in about 15 minutes | Servings 8)

Ingredients

1 box rice pudding mix

1/4 teaspoon ground cinnamon

A pinch of salt

2 cups nonfat milk

1 cup dried dates, pitted and chopped

1/4 cup cashews, chopped

Directions

First of all, prepare the rice pudding according to the manufacturer's instructions; add the cinnamon, salt, and milk; stir well to combine.

Spoon the pudding mixture into 8 dessert glasses; top with dates and cashews. Set in a refrigerator before serving time. Serve chilled and enjoy!

Festive Berry Pie

(Ready in about 1 hour 10 minutes | Servings 8)

Ingredients

For the Crust:

1 ¾ cups all-purpose flour

1/4 teaspoon cardamom

1/4 teaspoon cinnamon

1/8 teaspoon salt

3/4 cup butter, cold

1/2 cup cold water

1/2 teaspoon vanilla extract

1 large-sized egg, lightly beaten

For the Filling:

1 cup golden cherries

1 cup strawberries

1 cup blueberries

4 tablespoons agave nectar

1/2 stick butter, softened

Directions

In a mixing bowl, combine the flour, cardamom, cinnamon, and salt. Cut in the butter; the mixture should resemble coarse crumbs.

Pour in the water; add vanilla extract and egg. Cover and refrigerate the dough overnight.

The next day, divide your dough into two balls. Press one ball of the dough down evenly into the pie plate.

To prepare the filling, combine all the ingredients for the filling.

Preheat your oven to 350 degrees F; pour prepared filling into the pie crust. Roll out the second ball of dough; then top the pie with the second crust.

Brush the pie with an egg yolk. Bake your pie about 55 minutes. Transfer to a cooling rack before serving. Cut into wedges and enjoy!

Download PDF file with photos below:

Made in the USA
San Bernardino, CA
05 February 2017